I'm Special

And Other Lies We Tell Ourselves

Ryan O'Connell

Simon & Schuster Paperbacks
New York London Toronto Sydney New Delhi

Simon & Schuster
1230 Avenue of the Americas
New York, NY 10020

Names and identifying details of some of the people portrayed in this book have been changed.

First Simon & Schuster trade paperback edition June 2015

For information about special discounts for bulk purchases, please contact Simon & Schuster Special Sales at 1-866-506-1949 or business@simonandschuster.com.

The Simon & Schuster Speakers Bureau can bring authors to your live event. For more information or to book an event contact the Simon & Schuster Speakers Bureau at 1-866-248-3049 or visit our website at www.simonspeakers.com.

Interior design by Lewelin Polanco

Manufactured in the United States of America

10 9 8 7 6 5 4 3 2

Library of Congress Cataloging-in-Publication Data

O'Connell, Ryan.
I'm special : and other lies we tell ourselves / Ryan O'Connell. —
First Simon & Schuster trade paperback edition.
pages cm
1. Generation Y—Humor. 2. Conduct of life—Humor. 3. O'Connell, Ryan—Humor. I. Title.
PN6231.G385O36 2015
818'.602—dc23

2015003771

ISBN 978-1-4767-0040-3
ISBN 978-1-4767-0043-4 (ebook)

To Mom and Dad:

Thanks for fucking me up just the right amount.

Contents

I'm Special

Preface

HEY, MILLENNIALS! YOU NEVER thought for one second that this world wasn't meant for you to use, to exhaust, to squeeze the juices out of, did you? Your whole life you've been given the privilege to fuck up, to phone in the most important moments, to sleepwalk your way to your college diploma, and throw love away like a crumpled gum wrapper. Everyone is responsible for your vague anxieties, relationship ADD, lack of direction, and crippling fear of intimacy. Everyone is responsible for you but you. So take a bow and give thanks to everything that has made our generation possible. Give thanks to the Internet, texting, Skype, Snapchat, Vine, Instagram, Grindr, and Tinder for making face-to-face communication obsolete and terrifying. Give thanks to the loneliness that radiates from a bright computer screen and the sour surprise that comes from having hundreds of Facebook friends and not a single person to go to dinner with. Give thanks to your parents, who wanted to give you more, more, more. They showered you with affirmations and praise since their own parents never did it for them. Being a baby boomer meant that when they fell and scraped their knees, they found the Band-Aids on their own. It meant that they could disappear with their friends for hours without having to check in with dear old Mom. If our parents present their love to us in HD, our parents' parents decided to go in a more lo-fi direction.

Some people believe that part of being a parent is being able to give their child what they never had, and if that's the case, *this* is what the baby boomers must've lacked: Parents who acted as a pair of helicopters, hovering over their children every second of every day. Parents who poked, prodded, and engaged in the careful use of "I" statements when upset. Parents who not only bought Neosporin for you but practically lathered you in it from head to toe. The definition of what it means to be a good mom or dad has changed, and now we're all paying a special price for it one way or the other. By trying to shield their children from the messiness of life, our parents have created a generation that is bound to step in all of the dog shit.

Even if your parents took a more hands-off approach to raising you, you still could find other ways to be acknowledged. Ever since you signed up for that free trial of AOL with a dial-up modem in elementary school, you've been encouraged to share every brain fart, every hangover, every boring Saturday afternoon, so you do it! You share! Your latest tweet / status update, "Beautiful weather today. Going to eat a tuna sandwich. YUM," received six "likes" from borderline strangers, which means that people really do want to know what you're thinking all the time. They might not know it consciously but deep down they crave it. It's like a drug. HIT ME. HIT ME WITH YOUR COMMENTARY ABOUT THE WEATHER AND LOVE FOR TUNA SANDWICHES, PLEASE. I NEED IT.

You're special because whenever you date someone, you get to list yourself as "in a relationship" on Facebook. Showing your friends and acquaintances that you've finished first in the rat race for love is like giving yourself a virtual hand job, and every time a frenemy stalks your page and sees that you're taken, a little bit of your cum gets in their eye.

You're special because you have so many awards. You participated in a slew of extracurricular activities, and after each one came to an end, you were bestowed a meaningless superlative like "Most Spirited" or "Best Sense of Humor on the Kickball Team." Everyone got an award—it was the original version of No Child Left Behind—but yours held a greater weight than all the others. Afterward, you'd run home and place your new award next to your kindergarten diploma and a trophy you received for having the best ant farm in the second grade and then just sit back and smile, knowing that you were on the right track to success. Because the person who wins "Best Sense of Humor on the Kickball Team" doesn't become a fuckup. No, sir! They become astronauts, politicians, or, at the very least, a manager of a Sport Chalet. This was a sign that you were destined to do big things. Think about it. If you aren't going to be successful, who the hell is?

You're special because you have a blog. You're special because your father used to carry you to bed whenever you fell asleep on long car rides. You're special because your ex once made you a mixtape. You're special because you saw an Olsen twin at a concert once and she told you she liked your shoes. You're special because you get five OkCupid messages a day. You're special because an overweight balding man took your picture at a party and put it on his website. You're special because 212 people are following you on Twitter and you're only following 126. You're special because you did really well on the SATs and one of your teachers called you precocious. You're special because you grew up believing you could do anything you wanted and couldn't imagine thinking any other way. You're special because there are TV shows about you and your friends and because the *New York Times* won't stop publishing essays about twentysomethings. You're special because everyone is paying attention to your generation, wondering what kind of mark you'll make, and you like feeling noticed.

I know why you're special: because I'm special, too. In fact, if you looked up *Millennial* in the Urban Dictionary, you'd probably see a heavily filtered selfie of me. I've dipped my fingers in every cliché twentysomething pot imaginable. Helicopter parents who are obsessed with my every move? Check. A constant need for validation on the Internet? Check. An on-trend addiction to prescription pills? Sadly, check. I dated all the rotten boys, took all the internships that led to nowhere, drank all the wine, and swallowed all the drugs. I treated my life like it was a grand experiment, and then I had the audacity to be surprised when everything blew up in my face. Pretty dumb, right? Well, that's probably because, on top of being a typical young psycho, I'm retarded. No, really. I am. I was born with mild cerebral palsy (or, as I like to call it, cerebral lolzy), which means I walk with a limp and have little sprinklings of brain damage. So I'm not only special in the delicate snowflake kind of way, I'm also "riding the short bus" special! But despite my disability, I really am just like you. I'm someone who's trying to stop binging on poisonous penis and pad Thai delivery and learn how to actually, you know, love myself. It's not easy! Millennials have been told repeatedly that we're a giant failure of a generation and, unsurprisingly, many of us have started to believe it. But if you look back on history, you'll notice that every generation has been scrutinized and stereotyped—paging slacker Generation X and *Reality Bites*—so try not to sweat the criticism! Tell your insecurities to GTFO and just accept that our legacy might be a little un-chic. Once you do that, you can stop worrying about being the person the world expects you to be and start figuring out who it is you actually are. It may seem like an overwhelming journey, but I'll be right there with you. And if sharing any of my mistakes makes you feel less insane and alone, then I guess I don't regret anything I've done. Actually, that's not true. I regret running into oncoming traffic and getting hit by a car. But more on that later.

Growing Up Gimp

IN ORDER TO UNDERSTAND why you are the way you are, you must go back to the beginning and take a long, hard look at your family.

This is my family. This is where I come from.

My older sister, Allison (who, in her early twenties, renamed herself "Allisun," because you can do those kinds of things now and no one will even bat an eyelash), is a free-spirited vegan who is part of a small community of Hula-Hoopers in Brooklyn. (They call themselves "Hoopers," and they perform dances at Burning Man–like festivals. Some of them actually Hula-Hoop *for a living*.) "There's nothing cooler than being a Hooper," my sister told me one night while Hula-Hooping for me in her bedroom. She was using a hoop that had LED lights and retails for $360. "We're taking over!"

Although our five-year age gap prevented us from spending too much time together growing up, I do recall her being a part of some milestones in my life—the most important of which being the very first time my father learned that I might be gay. I was fourteen years old and still very much in the closet, but after my sister spent a semester at a liberal arts college, she came home one morning for Christmas break, took one look at me, and said, "You know you're gay, right?"

"No, I'm not!" I screamed at her, cleaning the dust off my Billie Holiday record and carefully putting it back in its case.

"It's okay, Ryan! Just be yourself!"

"Um, hello? I *am* myself. I don't think it's humanly possible to be anyone but me."

My father then walked into the room, rubbing the sleep from his eyes, and asked us what the hell was going on.

"Nothing, Dad."

"I'm telling Ryan that it's okay to be gay."

"Ryan's gay?" His face turned ghost white. Visions of his youngest son vogueing to Madonna and having anal sex danced in his head.

"No, I'm not. I promise!"

"Would it mean anything if he was?" my sister huffed. "I mean, I'm bisexual."

"You're what?"

"Yep." She smiled defiantly. "I have a girlfriend named Sky."

"Wait a second; I thought you had a boyfriend named John."

"I do. It's called being in a polyamorous relationship, Dad. Haven't you heard of it?"

"Oh Jesus. What is this bullshit? I'm going back to bed."

My father is a giant liberal teddy bear, but it's obvious that he comes from a very different generation than ours. When he decided to have kids, I don't think he even considered the possibility of having a bisexual polyamorous daughter and a gay son with a disability. We are modern as fuck.

My older brother, Sean, is also a textbook Millennial, but instead of changing his name and dating five people at the same time, he decided to take advantage of the invention of the Internet by making a porn website. When he was nineteen years old, Sean was broke and lived in a dilapidated apartment in Skid Row, a less than desirable part of LA, with limited career options. Then, in a moment of sheer desperation, he started a website that catered to his strengths, which happen to be finding the most disgusting pornos on the Web and editing them into disturbingly funny viral videos. His website is like Funny or Die but with homeless people fornicating in motel rooms set to a Björk song. It's absolutely disgusting, but in four years, he's managed to become a twentysomething millionaire. Welcome to America, babe!

And then, of course, there's me—the baby of the family and the most Millennial of them all. In the last few years, I've managed to make a career out of writing about being a hot mess, which is great but also not so great because I really *would* like to be stable at some point. Here I am, a person in my late twenties, and sometimes it feels like I'm so far from having my shit together. And I mean that literally. I do not even have my own feces together.

Allow me to explain. Recently, my mom, sister, and I decided to go to Montreal so we could eat bagels and create new painful memories together. I love going on vacation, even when it's with my family. The only downside is that I get severely constipated. When I was in the fifth grade, my brother and I went on a school camping trip to Big Basin for five days, and by the end of it, I hadn't taken a single shit. When we got home, my brother and I raced to the bathroom, and after we both finished doing our business, my brother looked at me and went, "Jesus. You didn't poop the entire time, either?"

Nothing's changed since then. It took three days and one unsavory experience of eating the disgusting Canadian delicacy poutine for my body to finally be like, "Okay, I feel safe enough to go number two now. Let's go!" As I raced to our rented apartment three blocks away from the restaurant, my mom and sister trailed behind me, stopping to take pictures of things white people like to immortalize on vacation, like street art, trees, and sidewalks. I was in the throes of pooping by the time they got back, and instead of leaving me to it, my mom knocked on the bathroom door.

"Ryan, are you okay?"

"I'm fine," I replied, my voice strained. "Be out in a minute."

That was a lie. The second I heard this poop smack the toilet water, I knew I was in deep shit. I got up and took a long breath before looking at my creation. It was huge. There was no chance in hell this sucker was going to make it down on its own, but against my better judgment, I decided to flush it anyway. You know when a poop is so big it doesn't even move? That's what this one did. It stayed exactly where it was, practically giving me the middle finger. Panicked, I muttered under my breath, "Holy fuck."

"What's going on in there?" my mom yelled through the door.

"Nothing, Mom. Just go away!"

"I'm coming in!" I scrambled to put my pants back on. When she entered the bathroom, she plugged her nose and screamed at me, "WHAT IN THE HELL DID YOU DO?"

"I clogged the toilet, but it's fine! I'll just use the plunger."

I looked. There was no plunger.

"Uh-oh."

My mom let out an exasperated sigh and made her way over to the toilet. She then took one look at the damage and said in all seriousness, "Honey, I didn't even know it was possible to have a poop that big." Part of me was flattered because it sounded like a compliment.

A few moments passed before my mom snapped into problem-solving mode and found some gloves underneath the sink.

"What are you doing?"

"There's no way that's going to go down. I need to take parts of your poop and put it in a trash bag."

"WHAT?" I exclaimed. "No, Mom—please don't do this. There must be an easier way."

"There isn't!"

"Well, at least let me do it!"

"No; now move over!"

There's really no way to accurately explain how it feels as

a twenty-six-year-old when you see your mother grab pieces of your poop and put it in a trash bag. Look, I am realistic about my goals as a human being. I know that growth doesn't happen overnight and that everyone's definition of what it means to be an adult is different. But by now I really thought my mom would have nothing to do with my poop. After all those years of providing shelter and cooking and caring for me, the least I could do for her is take care of my own literal shit.

But I can't do that. I can't do anything. My mom and dad raised three children, each one more special than the last, and this is what they've ended up with: a rich pornographer, a polyamorous Hula-Hooper, and a constipated mess. And although my family feels unique, I know we're not. In fact, I would put money on it and say that most of your parents would scoop up your shit out of a toilet if they had to. That's just the way things work now. This is what happens when you're a part of a generation that's raised by parents who don't want you to ever know struggle: you get a bunch of people in their twenties who never bothered to figure out how to live.

Most people my age were born under joyous circumstances: surrounded by family in the delivery room, someone gleefully capturing the birth with a video camera while everyone else crowds around the elated mother as she greets this blob of flesh for the first time. My birth, on the other hand, was an American Horror Story. The second I came out of my mother's vagina, I was blue and my brain was dying from lack of oxygen. The doctors told my parents that they had no way to predict the extent of my mental and physical impairments. There was no celebratory cake, no tender kisses—just pure "what the fuck just happened to our lives?" panic.

For the first few years, my parents lived in constant agony, not knowing if I was going to end up a total vegetable, let alone what other problems I was going to have. I didn't start walking until I was almost four years old, but apparently I've always been verbal. "You'd talk to anyone," my mom tells me. "You wouldn't shut up. It was hard to find it annoying, though, because it meant that your brain was actually working!" Gee, if you think about it, cerebral palsy is an ironclad defense for being a pest. "Mom and Dad, you need to put up with me because I could've been the human equivalent of a blank page!"

I wish I could say I was an easygoing, disabled butterfly who understood all the hardships my parents faced in raising a child with cerebral palsy, but I wasn't. In fact, I tortured them. They just made it so easy for me—especially my mom. "Ryan, let me wipe your face. Ryan, let me tie your shoes. Ryan, let me climb into your lungs and breathe for you because the thought of you having to do anything at all brings me such great pain." My entire generation was put under the care of a bunch of adults who would gladly frame their child's first solid bowel movement and shower them with accolades any time they didn't scream "FUCK YOU!" in their faces, so obviously the natural inclination was doubled when my mom gave birth to a kid who actually needed her permanent attention. I was fucked! She was fucked! My two siblings, who had been the king and queen of the castle until my high-maintenance ass showed up, were fucked!

Fearing that my mother and I were going to turn into a modern version of *Grey Gardens*, my father took it upon himself to become the anti–helicopter parent. With my mom, I always found a way out of doing something I didn't want to do, but my dad's bullshit detector was indestructible. He was immune to my manipulation and made sure I couldn't get away with anything, no matter how hard I protested or made my limp more pronounced. But whenever my dad laid down the law, my mother would try to lift it immediately. Take chores, for example. I'm pretty spastic, so sometimes when I would do something like use a broom at seven years old, I'd make an even bigger mess than there was to begin with. Instead of letting me just give up on it like everyone else would, my father would make sure I learned how to do it right—that is, until my mother would come waltzing in.

"What is this, Dennis?" my mom would bark, her face melting into a pool of sympathy as she saw me hopelessly trying to clean up something I had spilled on the floor.

"I'm teaching him how to use a broom, Karen!" my father would yell back. "He doesn't know how. Can you believe it?"

"Mommy," I would whimper, "I can't do it. It's too hard, and Dad won't let me go until it's finished."

"Did you hear that, Dennis? He can't do it! Now stop making him feel bad and let him go!"

"Yes, he can. He can't just walk away from everything without trying," he'd yell. "Ryan, focus on the broom!"

"Ryan, come to me!" she'd beckon, her arms outstretched. I'd move toward her.

"Don't even think about it, mister! Get back here right now."

"Don't listen to Daddy. Come to me!"

Sometimes my father would win and successfully force me to finish the chore. Sometimes he'd lose. No matter the outcome, though, my parents would end up furious at each other. Would you be surprised if I told you they filed for divorce when I was eight? No, of course you wouldn't, because everyone's parents are divorced now. Save for the occasional memory of my parents fighting over me, I don't even really remember mine being together. All I know is our family was in trouble before they'd split—we'd filed for bankruptcy and our house was in foreclosure. It was a place we were never able to afford, nestled in the hills of suburbia with a deck in the backyard that overlooked a sprawling barranca. We moved there because my sister was getting teased in our old neighborhood and my parents wanted to live somewhere she could make friends. It may seem like an extreme reaction to bullying, but this is a normal thing to do now. A child gets teased by her neighbor, so her parents sell the house and move into one they can't pay for. Duh.

I love my mom and dad, though. So much. My mom, in particular, was just born to be a mom. She's that good. Even though I've been financially independent from my parents for years, my mom and I share a bank account so she can write my checks and make sure my bills get paid on time. She also handles my taxes and deals with any issues I have with my health insurance. I tell myself that I let her do these things because it makes her feel needed, but I'm also just a spoiled brat who's used to having things done for him. And you'd think with all this codependency I would be calling my mom 24/7, but I'm not. In fact, when we do talk, the conversation usually goes something like this:

"Hi, honey," my mom coos into the phone. "What are you doing?"

"Nothing," I say curtly. "Actually, I'm, uh, really busy. What's up?"

"Oh, just doing some housework. So today I was at the post office and this annoying woman was in front of me with a package, and you wouldn't believe—"

"Mom, I have to go. Sorry."

"What? Why?"

"I'm swamped with work," I tell her. I'm actually Googling pictures of Kirsten Dunst and Jake Gyllenhaal from when they were a couple in the early 2000s.

"You can't even talk to me for a second?"

"Uh, no."

Then she starts to sound sad and then I get annoyed that she's sad and the conversation ends on a sour note. Then the strangest thing happens. I become racked with guilt and immediately want to call her back to say, "Oh my God, Mom. I love you so much. I'm sorry for that last conversation. Please finish your story about the woman in the post office. I must know how it ends!"

How does one go from feeling complete annoyance to overwhelming obsession in the click of a dial tone? A lot of my friends also have the same kind of contradictory relationship with their parents. We're *obsessed* and can't live without them. We're so happy that we have perspective now and can apologize for how badly we treated them when we were teenagers. But, *oh my God, they're calling me and I just can't deal with hearing their voice right now. I really was just looking forward to having an easy day with no drama, you know? Love them so much, though. I hope they still keep calling me so I can ignore it and feel loved!* My mother is my lifeline and I love her a scary amount, but sometimes when I talk to her, I can't help but feel like it's going at the pace of a Sofia Coppola movie.

Ironically, my father—the one who always held back from me when I was younger—is now my best friend. We go on vacations together. We hold hands when we walk down the street. In fact, I call him more than he calls me. So the moral of the parenting story seems to be that if you create a distance with your child, they'll grow up wanting your approval and become enamored with you. However, if you do everything for them and love them more than anyone else possibly could, they're going to ignore your phone calls. WTF?

Shortly before my parents announced that they were getting divorced, they combined forces one last time to drop a bombshell on me.

"Ryan, you need to have surgery. Major surgery."

"What do you mean?" I screamed at them. "Am I going to die?"

"No, honey," my mom said. "You aren't going to die."

"Well, Karen, it is an intense operation . . ."

"Dennis, stop!" My mom turned to me. "You need to have an Achilles tendon–lengthening surgery."

"And a femoral derotational osteotomy."

"What does that mean?"

"It means you're going to have to be in a wheelchair for three months, sweetie."

"Three months in a wheelchair? I can't!"

"Honey, you have no choice," my mom said. "I'm sorry."

"Oh, also kiddo, you're going to have to be in a full-body cast for two weeks," my father said.

Oh my God. This is the secret life of the mildly disabled child. We play in the sandbox, we have friends at school, and then we tell everyone, "BRB. Gotta go be in a full-body cast for a bit. Have a great summer!" I hated it. When you're older, you actively look for ways to stand out. If I got into a body cast today for two weeks, I would just laugh, take ten thousand pictures of it on Instagram, and watch the "likes" rack up. But when you're seven years old, the differences are your undoing. We're conditioned to ignore the things that make us ourselves and want nothing more than to disappear into a sea of bland and trendy clothing labels.

My time in a full-body cast was spent in my bedroom with the blinds drawn and channeling Jimmy Stewart in *Rear Window*, but I still had to go back to school in a wheelchair. Luckily, my parents had spent every last dime of their money on enrolling me in a small Episcopalian school where the average class size was fifteen, just so I could have closer relationships with my peers and minimize the risk of dealing with assholes. I went to St. Paul's in Ventura, California, from preschool to eighth grade and grew up with my classmates. We became a tight dysfunctional family, and even though we were occasionally rude to one another, no one made fun of me for my disability. Well, except this one time a girl ridiculed me for drooling on her during art class, but her own sister had cerebral palsy, so her taunts must've been coming from a place of dark insecurity, right?

Still, I dreaded going back to school in a wheelchair. I had no problem with being the special retarded son at home, but at St. Paul's, I wanted to be like everybody else. I had spent so much of my time making sure that my life with cerebral palsy didn't bleed into my life at school. Miraculously it worked! If I made people laugh, I could distract them from the fact that I was wearing leg braces and ran like Forrest Gump. But after school, I was confronted with the reality of my body's limitations. Physical therapy, endless doctor appointments, painful stretches when I got home—these were things I wanted to keep hidden from my friends, because once they knew all of the weird daily routines I had to go through, I was worried they would actually pity me. Pity doesn't buy friendship. Pity gets you uninvited to every birthday party past the fifth grade.

On the first day of school, I came squeaking up the wheelchair ramp the school had installed just for me and realized pretty quickly that most seven-year-olds are obsessed with things they don't understand. They treated my wheelchair like it was a foreign spaceship and fought over who got to push me to recess. When we got to the playground, they spun me around in circles and popped wheelies. I was delighted by all the attention because it meant my friends still liked me! They really, really liked me! When I finally got out of the wheelchair, a classmate assumed the role of a physical therapist and helped me relearn how to walk on the playground. The goal was to be able to reach the wall at the end of the playground without using my walker, and I actually did it! I made it to the wall, and everyone in my class—all fifteen of them—started clapping and cheering for me. Isn't that such a touching scene? Being nice as a kid is no easy feat. Their brains haven't fully developed yet, so they say all kinds of fucked-up shit to you like, "Why are you fat? Why is your face weird? Why are you so annoying?" My classmates at St. Paul's deserve medals for not behaving like little monsters toward me.

For high school, I went to a brand-new magnet school called Foothill Tech that might as well have been called Special Snowflake High. It was a place specifically designed for nerds and people with lots of feelings. The administration banned sports, choosing instead to highlight academic achievements, which meant that instead of going to a pep rally to root for an upcoming sports game, we had events called Renaissance Rallies where we gave awards to people on the honor roll. The students were smart. Sure, most of them had severe cystic acne, were socially inept, and suffered from involuntary erections during AP Calculus, but they were popular misfits—the antibully, if you will. When I started high school, I was a closeted gay guy with a limp who wore different-colored pairs of shoes. Anywhere else, I would've had a bull's-eye attached to my forehead, but at Foothill Tech I was just another freak. In fact, I was better than a freak. I was cool. No one was going to fuck with me. In the history of my four years at Foothill Tech, there was only one recorded fight on campus, and it was over a zip disc.

Strangely enough, the teachers at my high school were often weirder than the students. My English teacher was a female bodybuilder from South Africa who wore a *Star Trek* uniform to school and insisted that we all call her Captain Peterson. No one even thought to question her bizarre request, because at Foothill Tech, it was understood that everyone got to be an individual. When I came out of the closet my senior year of high school, they practically threw me a Welcome Homo party. Not only did I have a bunch of aspiring fag hags lining up to have me as their gay best friend, I also became more popular with the teachers. A few months after I came out, my teacher, Ms. Walker, who couldn't have been older than twenty-five, stopped me as I was leaving her class to ask me some, uh, unprofessional advice.

"Hey, Ryan," she called out. "Can you stay behind for a sec?"

"Sure," I mouthed back, assuming that I was getting in trouble for something.

When all my classmates had cleared out of the room, Ms. Walker sat on top of her desk and said to me, "Okay, so you're gay, right?"

"Um, yes . . ."

"Great! So my ex-boyfriend left me a voice mail—I haven't spoken to him in *years*, mind you—and I was wondering if you could listen to it and tell me what you think."

"Think about what, Ms. Walker?"

"Him getting into contact with me again!"

"Is this, like, for extra credit?"

"No, silly! I just would like your input, you know, as a gay guy."

"Okay . . ."

She played me the voice mail, and it sounded super vague

and noncommittal. After it was over, she looked at me excitedly, waiting for my answer.

"I don't know, uh . . ."

"Doesn't it sound like he wants to get back together?"

It did not sound like that. "Yes. Definitely."

"That's what I thought!" Ms. Walker rolled her eyes and let out a sigh of relief. "Thanks, babe. You're the best. You can go to your next class now."

Throughout the year, Ms. Walker acted like my BFF, gossiping with me after class and gifting me with mix CDs, one of which included a photo of her face on the cover. When I started falling behind in her class, I lied and told her I was going through a terrible breakup.

"FUCK HIM!" she screamed. "He's making a mistake. I swear, Ryan, if you weren't gay, I would be so in love with you."

Ms. Walker illustrates a key difference between my generation and my parents. If you came out of the closet in the 1970s, you'd end up a social pariah, but in the 2000s you have teachers celebrating the fact that you love the D. A school like Foothill Tech signaled an important shift in teaching styles and the accepted social order for the Millennial generation. Gone were the days of being popular just because you played sports and had a six-pack or put out. Now your popularity is measured by how special and weird you are.

Before Foothill Tech, my disability would try to get me to acknowledge it and I'd be like, "What? Um, I don't know you. Bye!" By the time I was a sophomore, however, I was making small steps to embrace my differences. As part of a graduation requirement, Foothill Tech made each of its students complete seventy-five hours of community service. Most kids volunteered to spread the word of Jesus Christ to vulnerable In-N-Out Burger customers everywhere, but I decided to be bold and work with United Cerebral Palsy of Los Angeles. My responsibilities there would include hanging out at disabled kids' houses and chaperoning the occasional field trip. It sounded so chill and relaxed. While all my friends were busy cleaning up dead whale parts on the beach for community service, I would be getting credit just to hang out with my mongoloid people! (I can say mongoloid because I am one, right? That's usually how it works, isn't it—people reclaiming the power of the offensive word and making it theirs? Babe?)

But I quickly realized that I might have made a mistake in my quest to become the gay Mother Teresa. My first task involved taking twenty kids with cerebral palsy to the harbor, and it turned out to be a complete fucking disaster. Even though I was with licensed physical therapists who were helping me manage the kids, I still had to watch them like a hawk, because the second I turned my back, they'd be ready to jump off the goddamn pier to go for a swim. The whole day consisted of me frantically running around and catching them moments before they did something that could've killed them. It felt like the blind leading the blind or, in this case, the less retarded leading the more retarded.

A week later, I was driven to a boy's house in Thousand Oaks, where I was told to simply spend time with him and play video games. "Perfect," I thought. "I'm great at hanging out!" When I got to the house, his mother, who seemed like a very nice Valley girl-woman, led me to his bedroom.

"Dustin," she squealed, "your friend is here to play with you."

Dustin didn't even bother to turn around and say hello to me, although who could blame him? There's something especially humiliating about having to get a volunteer to hang out with you. Undeterred, I sat down next to him on the floor and asked what he was playing.

"*Twisted Metal 2,*" he responded blankly. His speech was a little slow and slurred in a way that I later found to be similar to someone who was high on heroin.

I watched Dustin destroy cars in a field for half an hour until he finally paused the game and acknowledged my existence.

"Why is your hair blue?" he asked.

It was actually a really good question. Why *was* my hair blue? Oh, right—because when I met Dustin I was still in the closet and the only way I could express my sexuality was by dyeing my hair unfortunate colors. I didn't know that at the time, though, so I just explained to him that I did it because it seemed fun.

"Oh," he said. "Are you going through puberty?"

"Um, I guess." My neck stiffened up. "I, uh, kind of already went through that."

"Do you have a girlfriend?"

"No."

"Do you have a lot of friends?"

"Yeah, I do."

"What do you guys do for fun?"

"Just, you know, normal stuff. Go to the movies and hang out at each other's houses. Nothing too crazy."

"Oh."

A look of embarrassment spread across Dustin's face that let me know just how different my definition of "normal" was from his.

"What do you do for fun?" I asked him, already knowing the answer.

"Play video games."

"What else?"

"I don't know." He paused. "Nothing."

Dustin then resumed play on his video game and ignored me for the rest of our playdate. After I left his house, I never worked with UCPLA again. Spending time with other kids who had CP was supposed to give me a sense of belonging, but in the end it just made me feel even more alienated. The people I met had trouble talking, which prevented us from having any kind of meaningful dialogue, so most of the time I would just sit there and occasionally help them accomplish menial everyday tasks or make sure they didn't electrocute themselves. On one hand, I wanted to help these disabled kids and offer them my friendship, but on the other, I selfishly wanted them to be *my* friend and offer *me* support. When they had trouble doing that, I felt let down and annoyed, which, in turn, made me feel like a self-serving dick. Who was I to get mad at some kid for not being able to hold a conversation with me because he had severe brain damage?

I just wanted to find a friend who was like me, someone I could commiserate with about drooling all over myself and being terrible at sports. I imagined conversations that went something like "Hey, isn't it the worst when you're walking somewhere and lose your balance for no reason and just fall?

Ha ha, it's awful! Or how about when it takes you twenty minutes to figure out how to put a key in a lock because you have poor hand-eye coordination? I hate it when that happens!" But I couldn't find that companionship, and I left every experience feeling more guilt and shame about my disability than before.

I thought I could be close to someone just because we had something in common. Growing up, you're always looking for things to define you, to tell you what you are, because you aren't able to figure it out on your own yet. Some people join an organized religion, sew their pants up with dental floss, or smoke pot just to make a connection, so I suppose hanging out with a disabled kid in Thousand Oaks doesn't actually seem that radical by comparison. Still, what do you do when you can't find that one person who makes you feel not so different? In my case, you retreat. After the disappointing experience with UCPLA, I swiftly went back into my disabled shell and was certain no one would ever understand what it felt like to have one foot in the world of cerebral palsy and one foot in this "normal able-bodied" life. I continued to play the Special card at home with my family while hiding it from everybody at school. By now, I was perfect at knowing how to hide the wrinkles. People would only see what I wanted them to see.

It's been over a decade since I've worked with UCPLA and tried to keep my disability on the DL, and I've got to tell you: it's a full-time job keeping the two worlds separate. There's a point that comes in everybody's life when you have to stop denying the things that make you different and start to accept what you've been given—even if what you've been given is embarrassing, ugly, and prone to drooling involuntarily on people. So no more lies, no more bullshit: this is what it's been like for me to have cerebral palsy in a generation where every person is treated slightly special to begin with.

Number one: people will think you have more brain damage than you actually do. My high school guidance counselor, for example, thought I was a Grade A retard when, at best, I was only a Grade C or D. Whenever I went to talk to her, she fawned over me like I was the boy in the bubble.

"Good tooooo seeeeee youuuuu, Ryan," she greeted me one day. "Are you getting along okay?"

"Um, yeah; I'm fine. I just need to switch out of AP Government. I'm not even planning to take the AP test, so it's just a waste of my time, you know?"

"Okay, okay, I hear what you're saying, but tell me what's really going on. Is the course moving too fast for you?" She placed a reassuring hand on my arm and gave me "I care" eyes.

"No, I get it. I got an A on the last pop quiz. To be honest, I just hate the teacher. She gives us tons of busy work, and I feel like I'm not learning anything."

"Is she not accommodating your needs? She knows you're allowed extra time on tests, right?" Even though she was acting sweet, I just wanted to punch her in the face. Being treated like a retard is only beneficial at places where you get to skip the lines, like the airport, the DMV, and Disneyland. Everywhere else just feels cruel.

"I don't need more time on tests. Have I ever needed it? I just want to be placed in regular Government."

"I'm going to talk to your teacher and make sure she's aware of your special situation."

"But—"

"Ryan, you've come too far to cheat yourself now. Even though you have some limitations, I really believe that with the proper adjustments, you can really excel at AP Government. Have a good day and come back to visit me if you're still not getting the hang of it, okay?"

And that was that. I was shooed out of her office, my request denied. I didn't get it. Shouldn't I get taken out of AP *because* I have brain damage? It's like my guidance counselor adopted me as her personal pet project and was determined to save me from underachievement. I could just imagine her going home to her husband after work and being like, "Oh my God, I have the sweetest student with cerebral palsy. He's slow with certain things, but I'm not going to give up on him, dammit!" It's an admirable goal, but she neglected to find out if anyone had given up on me in the first place.

Number two: people will assume you're wasted when you're actually stone-cold sober. Once, I ran into an acquaintance at a party and we talked casually for a few minutes before I left to go home. The next time I saw him, he was like, "Dude, do you remember seeing me at that party a while ago?" Confused, I responded, "Of course I remember. Why wouldn't I?" Then, pretty much screaming in my face, he explained, "Because you were wasted! When I saw you, it looked like you could barely walk, man!"

Oops—guilty as charged! It's just my limp. Bouncers at bars have gone so far as to give me the stare down and ask my friends, "Is he okay?" before letting me in, insinuating that I appear to be totally fucked-up. Seven point five times out of ten, though, I'm completely sober! When people accuse me of being drunk, I'm so mortified that I just choose to go along with it. "Man, you're right," I'll say sheepishly. "I was out of control that night. I'm sorry. Did I do anything super embarrassing?"

Number three: people will assume that you must have just gotten into a terrible accident. I learned this when I decided to be an accident victim for Halloween and walked down Santa Monica Boulevard in nothing but a hospital gown. (It was my interpretation of a slutty Halloween costume. Most people would either be a lifeguard or Tarzan if they wanted to show off their body, but I figured that since I already had a limp, why not expose my ass in a flimsy hospital gown and splatter fake blood on my face?) Unfortunately, my "costume" backfired when four drivers stopped by the side of the road to ask me if I needed to get to a hospital.

Number four: people will make jokes about cerebral palsy without knowing you actually have it. This happened to me at a gay bar, of all places, and it was completely traumatizing. I was flirting with some guy and we were playing this game where you arbitrarily identify things as being '80s, '90s, or millennium. (For example, minifridges are so '80s, whereas having a gluten allergy is very millennium.) Things were going so well at first. We were laughing and drinking and giving each other "I'm going to fuck you later and only regret 22 percent of it!" eyes. But then all of a sudden, the dude says to me, "Oh, I got a good one! Cerebral palsy is sooooo '80s."

Ha ha—wait, WHAT? Did the words *cerebral palsy* just come out of this boy's mouth? Rewind the tape! Oh damn, there it is in slow motion: "Cereeeeeebral palllllsy is sooooo '80s." Fuck me. Here was this cute guy who was most likely going to sleep with me in two hours and he makes a joke about a disability he doesn't even know I have. I was so shocked that I just laughed uncomfortably and quickly moved the game along by adding, "Uh, yeah. What about scoliosis? I think that's pretty '90s." If I were a braver soul, I would've said something like this:

Me: Hey, jerkface!

Boner Killer: Yeah, babe?

Me: I have cerebral palsy and I can definitely say that it's not '80s. It's very today! Haven't you seen *Breaking Bad*?

Boner Killer: Um, no.

Me: Well, there's a major character with CP on it. So, in case you were wondering, my disability is very on-trend. It's not like I have polio or something!

Boner Killer: Okay, babe.

Me: And you were probably going to get to see me naked in a few hours and receive a fairly adequate blow job! But now you won't! Now you have to go home and jack off by yourself! So bye!

Boner Killer: Bye, babe.

Me: Wait—do you still want my number?

Boner Killer: . . .

But since I'm neither cool nor well adjusted, I had to settle on having one more awkward drink and hightailing it back home in a cab so I could watch episodes of *Breaking Bad* on Netflix to feel better about my situation. I was pissed. Sex was within my grasp, but one joke about people who limp ended up giving me a limp dick. What's even more sickening is that it gave me a sense of pride knowing that I had successfully fooled him into thinking that I was able-bodied. Whenever I meet a cute boy, there are certain tricks I use to conceal my limp. In a bar, it's easy because I'm mostly sitting down, and on the off chance that I have to stand, I can just lean against something. Then, if we actually (gasp!) walk to the front of the bar or the back patio, I make sure to always walk behind the person a little bit so they don't see me limping. I'm like a disabled magician, except it's less magic and more tragic.

Number five: people stare. A lot. Even when I lived in New York—a place that proudly ignores both celebrities and stab victims—people would do a double take when they saw me limping toward them. It's especially confusing when a cute gay boy is doing it. Sometimes my friends will inform me when someone is checking me out, but most of the time I think they're just staring at my hunchback. This is a terrible thing to assume, but when you grow up with small children looking at you and then asking their parents, "WHAT'S WRONG WITH THAT MAN?" you become a little jaded. That's why I'm never sure a guy is actually into me until they're actually putting their dick into my ass. And even then I'm like, "Really? Are you sure? There's still time to back out!" I'd like to think that I have healthy self-esteem when it comes to the way I look. I see myself in the mirror and think, "You're cute, funny, and smart. I get why people might want to give all their love and genitalia to you." But when it comes down to actually pursuing a crush or getting ready to have sex, I feel a little shocked when the feelings are reciprocated. "This sexy able-bodied person is willing to have sex with someone who has a disability? Wow—they're a great person. I don't know if

I would do that if I were in their position!" I shouldn't feel so honored whenever someone wants to sleep with me—and I don't all the time. Sometimes I definitely feel like I'm the one doing the person a favor, but oftentimes I do feel lucky. I just can't fathom why someone would be with me when they can be with someone who can have Cirque du Soleil sex and go on bike rides with them and climb ladders to fun rooftop parties and stick their legs up in the air for long periods of time.

Number six: some people think you're in a lot of pain. One of the things I get annoyed with the most is when I fall in public—which happens a lot—and people act like it's the JFK assassination. Strangers swarm over me and ask worried questions like, "Are you okay? OMG, can you feel from the waist down?" When I get up and assure them that I'm okay, they see that I'm limping and start to really freak out. "Dear God, you're limping! We need to get you to a hospital!" Then I have to explain to them that I've always walked this way, which leads to an even bigger upset. A disabled person who fell? It can't be! By the end of the whole debacle, I'm the one consoling *them*.

Sometimes I wonder if I had been born with cerebral palsy during the baby boomer era whether I'd be left alone. There would be no guidance counselor treating me like a five-year-old, no people stopping on the side of the road to ask if I need to go to the hospital, no parents hovering over my every move. Right before I left my small beach town for college in San Francisco, I figured this would be my chance to start over and become someone less defined by my disability. I started over, all right. Just not how I expected to.

Getting Hit by a Car

(and Other Amazing Things That Can Sometimes Happen to You if You're Really Lucky!)

IS THERE ANY WORSE possible time to be a human being than during your freshman year of college? The personal transformation you undergo is startling. You leave your hometown feeling mature and ready to tackle independence with gusto, but then the second you set foot on campus, you regress into a beer-swilling nightmare. Gone are any goals of taking an 8:00 a.m. class and joining a feminist study group. You just want to have fun, make out with people you hate, and puke.

College is about figuring out who you are, and in order to do that, you need to become a lot of people you aren't. It's about reinvention. Since you're far away from everything and everyone you know, you have the opportunity to become the person you weren't allowed to be in high school. You're not living up to anyone's expectations anymore. You have the freedom to do whatever the hell you want.

After I graduated from my Future #Blessed Millennials of America high school, I went to San Francisco State University, where I realized pretty quickly that I had no idea how to live without my parents' guidance. At eighteen years old, I still didn't know how to do laundry or cook or clean. I was so desperate for help that I began giving weed to this girl on my dorm floor in exchange for cleaning my room. But as terrifying as it was to live on my own, I was excited to start over. I didn't know a single person at school, which might've seemed scary for anyone else, but I saw it as an amazing opportunity to become something more than the gay gimp I was in Ventura. Unfortunately, a change in geography did little to change my circumstances. At college, people would still look at me like, "Uh, there goes that flamboyant homo who walks like a ninety-year-old man!" Meanwhile, everyone around me was exploding with change. The first friend I made at school, Stephanie, came to college untainted, all smiles and getting tipsy off two bottles of Mike's Hard Lemonade. Then, after a few months, she tried her first line of cocaine, loved it, and was gone, baby, gone. Reinvention isn't always synonymous with growth. Sometimes it's just about letting go and becoming the worst possible version of yourself.

When Stephanie fell too far down the K hole of cocaine, I searched for a new friend and stumbled upon a gay mini–Patrick Bateman named Evan. When I first tried talking to him at school, he ignored me because I was wearing ugly cowboy boots and had dried toothpaste all around the edges of my mouth. Then, like every smart Millennial, he went home, stalked me on every social network, discovered we had mutual friends, and decided I was cool enough to talk to.

"Hey, Ryan," Evan greeted me warmly one day when I was on my way to the dining hall. He moved in to give me a hug.

"Uh, hi, Evan . . ."

"So listen, I just went on your Facebook and saw that you're, like, really good friends with Wyatt."

"Yeah; we went to high school together. How do you know him?"

"He's close with this guy I'm kind of seeing in New York. Wyatt's really cool. We hung out together at Misshapes." Misshapes was a popular nightclub in New York that was frequented by sociopaths with eating disorders. I went there once and left because it made me feel like a sad, hipster version of Kirstie Alley.

"Awesome. I freaking love Misshapes."

"Yeah, so we should hang out sometime."

"Definitely. I would like that. Call me."

Evan and I became inseparable after that day, sneaking into bars together, gossiping, and watching marathons of trashy reality TV. I don't know why I felt so honored to be in his presence. I didn't even really like him. He gave me strong "BAD PERSON WHO WILL RUIN YOUR LIFE!" vibes, but I ignored it because I was desperate for any kind of closeness. As it happens, Evan did turn into a complete asshole after we became friends. He began to put me down, make disparaging comments about my appearance, and try to control my social life. It was like having an emotionally abusive boyfriend but without the mind-blowing sex.

"Where are you right now?" Evan texted me one night. Beads of sweat started to form on my forehead because I was at a restaurant he hated with people he didn't like. I contemplated lying to him so he wouldn't make fun of me for it, and sometimes I actually did lie, but this time I decided to be brave and tell the truth.

"At Park Chow with Caitlin," I texted back.

"Ew. That's embarrassing."

"Wanna hang out later?" I frantically wrote, hoping to quell his annoyance.

No response. After sending him a few more desperado texts that said some variation of "I'm sorry! I'll be done really soon. Let's hang, please!" he acquiesced and said, "Fine, I guess. Come over." I wolfed down dinner, said good-bye to my friend, and rushed to his apartment, where I spent the next few hours getting ridiculed for hanging out with "lame people." Sometimes, in a bizarre act of repressed gay aggression, we'd wrestle. Then I went home and we did the same thing all over again the next day.

Most of us have been in a toxic friendship before. We've had that person in high school or college who latches on to our insecurities and plays them like a fiddle. It's almost like an addiction. This person brings you down and instead of trying to get back up, you lay there asking for the next kick. That's what happens when you don't know who you are yet: you let someone else decide for you.

Evan and I were "BFFs" for two twisted years. Eventually I was able to muster up the courage to kick him to the curb—but not before something happened that restored most of my confidence and allowed me to reinvent myself. I didn't find my new identity by changing my style or doing drugs or getting into an all-consuming relationship like everyone else had done in college. It was easier than that. All I had to do was get hit by a car.

A downside to having cerebral palsy is that sometimes your brain will decide to take a nap and screw you forever. When people ask me why I decided to run into oncoming traffic on May 9, 2007, I don't know what to tell them other than, "Oops. My bad. I'm retarded." Sometimes my brain will black out and I'll lose all capability of making a proper decision. That's what happened when, during finals week of my sophomore year at San Francisco State, I ran into oncoming traffic to try to catch a bus that was going back to school.

I remember some things about the accident, like the sound of tires screeching and everything going black. I came to with an elderly woman standing over me, asking if I was okay. I told her yes, tried to get up, and immediately fell back down. An ambulance came, and I tried to explain to the EMTs that this couldn't be happening to me. I had to go back to school and take my Coloring Queer final (yes, that was a real class I took). "Sit still," an EMT scolded me. "You're going to hurt yourself even more if you keep moving around."

I had been living under the assumption that bad things didn't happen to gay people with cerebral palsy, but a few moments after arriving in the ER, my condition worsened when I lost the ability to move and feel my left hand. One second I was doing jazz hands on the gurney and the next it was totally frozen. "It's just a nerve contusion," one doctor assured me. "You'll regain movement and sensation in a few days."

After two days and a series of misdiagnoses, it was revealed that I had compartment syndrome—a semi-rare condition that can develop after the body experiences trauma to a compartment of muscles. When that car smashed into my elbow at 45 mph, it caused pressure to develop in my forearm that was cutting off the oxygen supply to my muscles. This can result in a whole boatload of things, including amputation, but for me it meant a permanent, major loss of function in my left hand. Eight years after my accident, I've undergone six surgeries and had a skin graft. I can't handwrite, tie my shoes, or give decent hand jobs (although, to be fair, who knows if I ever could). Basically, I am just a little more disabled than I was before. And even though I've never been totally able-bodied—I've never walked without a limp, I've never been flexible—my condition before the accident seemed manageable because I never knew anything different. This, however, was something else. This felt like the world was robbing someone who didn't have much to begin with.

After leaving the hospital, I moved to Los Angeles and took the semester off from school to recover. Sensing that I might be spiraling into a depression, my dad sent me to a gay shrink. "He'll empathize with you more," my dad explained as he drove me to my first appointment. "You know, because he also likes dudes." I arrived at my shrink's office—which was on the corner of Cock Ring and Poppers in West Hollywood—not knowing what to expect, but I immediately became suspicious when I saw a sexy glamour head shot of my therapist in the waiting room. "That's strange," I thought to myself. "Do therapists normally take sensual head shots?" Shrugging it off, I entered his office and laid eyes on the man who was going to bring me catharsis.

Holy shit. No, no, no. This can't be right. My shrink, Adam, was stunningly gorgeous. He had piercing blue eyes, a sleek haircut, and was wearing one of those sophisticated outfits that was supposed to be conservative but wasn't actually because it was a size too small and seemed to deliberately show off his spectacular gym body. My penis was doing jumping jacks at the mere sight of him, which is why I knew instantly that this wasn't going to work. I would never let myself open up and ugly-cry to someone that good-looking. Instead, I'd try to put on a show and pray that one day he would take pity, bend me over the couch, and screw the depression out of me. "Hey, Ryan." Adam shook my hand and motioned for me to sit down. "What brings you here today?"

"Um, not much," I stammered, suddenly self-conscious and pulling the hair out of my face.

"Not much?" Adam gave me a confused look before checking my file. "Your father told me you were hit by a car a month ago."

"Oh, yeah," I laughed nervously. "That. I guess things have been pretty heavy."

"Are you depressed? You've gone through a major life change, so I would expect you to be experiencing some feelings of despair right now."

"Maybe? Gosh, I don't know. Tell me about you! How long have you been a therapist?"

Adam paused and looked me dead in the eye. "How are you doing, Ryan? You can tell me. That's why you're here."

I shifted in his $10,000 leather chair and blurted out the first thing that came to mind. "Well, okay. If you really want to know, I'm convinced no one's ever going to want to have sex with me again."

"And why's that?"

"Because I have cerebral palsy and now I'm one-handed. Being with me would be like having sex with a fidgety lobster claw."

Adam smiled. He had great teeth. "Ryan, I can already tell that you're an attractive, bright individual. I guarantee you that you'll find someone."

"Really? You think I'm attractive?"

"Sure."

"And you think someone would actually want to see me naked after all of this mess?"

"Why not?"

"Wow, great!" I beamed before getting serious. "So do you know who specifically would sleep with me? Like, did you have anyone in mind or are you just speaking generally?"

"Um, generally, Ryan."

"Oh." I sunk back into my chair. Fantasies of us holding our adopted baby, Moppet Azul, on a safari in Africa were dashed to hell.

"So, besides feeling undesirable, is there anything else you're struggling with post-accident?"

"Um," I hesitated. *Don't let him see you sweat, Ryan. Keep it together. The goal is to make him like you.* "Nope; I think that about covers it!"

After our anticlimactic first session together (and having one amazing climax alone in my shower an hour later), I promised myself that I'd quit Adam and find a therapist who could actually help me sift through the wreckage in my brain. I could never go through with it, though. Spending time with him was like seeing a hint of a shirtless dancing rainbow in an otherwise hopeless sky. Adam was like my hooker, but instead of paying him to fuck me, I was giving him money to feed me compliments and hand me bottles of Fiji water. If insurance hadn't stopped covering our sessions, I probably would've seen him indefinitely.

Life in LA was not turning into the healing Namaste journey I thought it was going to be. Now that my weekly sessions with Adam were over, I had nothing to do. So I passed the time by eating. A lot. I ate at a Chipotle that was near my apartment four times a week. After devouring a giant burrito, I would then walk to a place called Sprinkles and order four cupcakes, two of which I would eat in a Kinko's parking lot on Elm and Wilshire. Besides treating my body like a carb Dumpster and deleting 461 days from my lifespan, I also got to know my roommate, Emma. The two of us had met at a house party a year earlier and immediately bonded over our love of astrology and pugs. When I moved to LA, Emma suggested we sublet a place together and I thought, "Why not? This girl seems fun, flirty, fabulous! I mean, we've only met IRL once, but I'm sure she's totally great!" A week into us living together, I realized I had made a grave error in judgment.

"Hey, babe," she bellowed one day when she entered our apartment carrying a $400 gym bag and her favorite Lululemon yoga pants. "You will not believe how much I just paid for an iced mocha at Urth Caffé!"

"How much?" I asked with the bare minimum of enthusiasm.

"FIFTEEN DOLLARS!" she exclaimed. "Can you believe it?"

"No, I can't. No iced mocha costs fifteen dollars. That's actually impossible."

"I'm not kidding. It really was fifteen dollars. The prices there are outrageous!"

She was right. The prices at Urth Caffé were outrageous, but there's still no such thing as a fifteen-dollar mocha. I was offended by how unabashedly false her lie was. She wasn't even striving for authenticity here.

"I really don't believe you. There's no way."

"Ryan, why would I lie?"

Now there's a question I would've loved an answer to. Emma did nothing *but* lie. She told me she was a nationally ranked tennis player, that she used to strip at Scores, that she had a sugar daddy who sent her money even though nothing sexual would ever happen between them, that Kat Von D tattooed her at a house party, that she was in training for Wimbledon. She was nuts, but her antics were a nice distraction from the pathetic happenings of my life. Whenever I thought I was losing my mind, I'd flash back to Emma and her delusions about fifteen-dollar mochas and instantly feel rooted in reality.

I needed all the pick-me-ups I could get. Acquiring another disability on top of the one I already had messed with my sanity and moved my self-esteem from "Sometimes I like myself on Tuesdays and Thursdays!" to "I am a disgusting Grendel whose penis might as well be donated to charity."

All my friends in San Francisco were busy moving in together and getting into serious relationships. They were constantly evolving, and even though the accident had given me the chance to start over, too, I was treating my beginning like a permanent ending.

The only way you can recover from a traumatic event is if you admit to yourself and others that you're miserable. People always feel this pressure to say that they're in such a good place when they're actually swimming in a bottomless pit of despair. In order to get past anything, you have to own your misery. You need to write, "THIS DEPRESSION IS THE PROPERTY OF: [insert your name here]." Otherwise, it's going to stick to you forever.

I lied to my friends about how I was doing, and I slept in a lot; my eyes felt sewed shut by my depression. When I did leave my apartment, I cried in public. I sampled everything on the grief buffet and went back for seconds. During my recovery, I had nothing but time to think about the difficult questions no one likes to give any thought to, like, What do people really want out of life? What keeps them content after their looks fade and they've seen loved ones die and they've been betrayed? Before you hit your mid- to late twenties, it's hard to think of yourself as someone who's in control of his life. It almost feels like your body is a loaner, something given to you to wreak havoc on. These bruises aren't yours. This weight gain isn't yours. None of it is real. You can go back to the way things were at the drop of a hat. You can reverse the damage with a good night's sleep. You can treat people terribly and expect them to still be there for you in the morning.

Getting hit by a car gave me my first taste of the things that were worth valuing. It made me realize how badly I wanted to get better and live a fully functional life so I could love somebody and have them love me back and be with my friends and family and do work that I was proud of and get a dog and lay in warm sheets and watch a matinee by myself and try using a cock ring and watch my best friend get married. I was starting to understand that nothing in this life is owed to me and that it's quite possible to sabotage yourself if you don't pay attention.

Of course, all these moments of clarity were brief—I still had many years of being a fuckup ahead of me—but they were strong enough to lift me out of my post-accident fugue. While living in LA, I applied and got accepted to Eugene Lang, a college in New York that's like NYU but with cheaper tuition and more flannel and cocaine. I was terrified to start a whole new life with a hand that was permanently out to lunch, but moving to New York actually turned out to be the step I needed to take to realize my accident had actually been a blessing in disguise.

When I went to Lang, I majored in creative writing because all I knew how to do was have feelings. Have you had the unique pleasure of taking a writing workshop at a liberal arts college? If not, let me explain how it works. Twenty students sit in a room and jizz all over themselves for an hour and a half. Then at the end of class, the teacher hands everyone a towel so they can wipe the cum off.

Okay, that's not really what happens. Students read their stories aloud, which are usually about Brooklyn house parties or genocide, and then they get workshopped—that is, your peers tear your story apart under the guise of giving you constructive criticism. The author will get defensive and sometimes cry and scream, assuring us that we just don't understand her vision, and then class is over.

The girls in a writing workshop usually have weird names like Sandstorm and Aura, and the dudes are usually gay. If, for some strange reason, they're straight, they worship Charles Bukowski, are functional alcoholics, and will sleep with half the girls in the class before the semester is over. My favorite kind of person in a writing workshop is the shy girl in the corner who doesn't say a word until it comes time to read her story, and then shit gets psycho.

"Ahem," she'll say, clearing her throat. Everyone looks over because they've never heard her speak.

"So this story is about a girl named Oxtail, and it's about rape. And molestation. Because I was raped and molested."

Everyone's jaw drops. She starts to read.

"Lick my pussy, you asshole. I was in the woods and it was dark but you found me and you grabbed my tits and I sucked your cock and together we were fucking under the moonlight. And then you offered me heroin and I said yes. So then we did heroin. Oh yeah. I'm on heroin. Feel my pussy. Go inside it. Fuck yeah. That feels good. No, wait. It feels terrible. What the fuck? ARE YOU MY DAD?"

By the time she's finished reading, the entire class is silent. The girl looks up, and just like that, she's back to her usual quiet self. "Um, thanks," she'll whisper before covering her face with a hoodie. Meanwhile, everyone is struggling to comprehend how something so dark could've come out of someone who wears Skechers.

You meet people with conflicting identities all the time in college. One half is the person they've always been and the other half is the person they're actively trying to become. It's exhausting. College kids aren't tired from staying up all night studying or partying. They're tired from not having the slightest idea who they are.

Going to Lang, I was prepared to give up on my quest to become another person and be honest about who I was: the cerebral palsy, the compartment syndrome—all of it. Then I went to a house party and realized I didn't have to.

"I don't mean to be rude, but . . . what happened to you?" a drunk girl asked me shortly after I moved to New York. In the background, kids were dancing to Jay Z and having heated discussions about white privilege.

"I got hit by a car," I told her, sipping from a red cup filled with warm white wine.

Her eyes widened and she covered her mouth in horror. "OH. MY GOD. I AM SO SORRY. HOW DID THAT HAPPEN?"

"I ran into oncoming traffic."

She scrunched up her nose and scoffed. Suddenly she wasn't so sympathetic. "Why in the hell did you do that?"

"I'm not really sure . . ." I trailed off. This was a story I was going to have to tell for the rest of my life, and I had better get a script figured out quick.

"Okay," she paused, waiting for me to proceed but when I didn't, she continued. "So, like, what actually happened?"

"I developed this thing called compartment syndrome and, um, well, it essentially fucked up my hand forever."

"Wait—your hand? I didn't even notice that."

For a brief moment, I was confused. How could she not have noticed my hand? What else was there to notice besides . . . oh. Right. There's that other thing I have.

"So did it crush your side, too, or . . . ?"

I thought about it for a second. Technically, the car did hit my right side. I even have a little scar on my ass from it. If I told her yes, I wouldn't really be lying. I'd just be neglecting to tell her the full story.

"Um, yeah. That's exactly what happened." I sighed. "That's why I have a limp. That's why all of this"—I motioned to my entire body—"is happening."

With that lie, I remade myself. I was no longer Ryan, the guy with cerebral palsy. I was Ryan, the accident victim.

After that night, I never spoke about my cerebral palsy to anyone. I chalked everything up to the accident and got the opportunity to live my life on the other side of the disabled coin. Can you blame me for doing some creative editing? For the first time in my life I was in possession of some confidence. Shortly after telling the drunk girl my little lie, I hooked up with a boy for the first time in two years. Ryan, the cerebral palsy sufferer, wasn't worthy of getting laid, but Ryan, the accident victim, was. I would walk up to cute boys, limp and all, and start chatting them up. If I had a crush on someone, I wouldn't hesitate to grab their face in the hallway of my apartment and start kissing them. I had officially thrown my disability into a garbage can on Third Avenue and exchanged it for clandestine make-outs, hazy sex, and a set of Cisco Adler balls. When you're twenty-one, twenty-two, and twenty-three, sex is constantly vibrating off your body and it doesn't matter if you're the hottest thing in the world. You're young, you're ripe, and you deserve to be picked. That attitude had infected all of my friends, but I had yet to experience it on my own. Now I wanted all the penis, all the love, all the experiences that came with being someone who likes himself.

This confidence continued to stick with me all throughout college, but eventually I found myself slowly regressing back into the insecure person I was before. As wonderful as it was to be able to leave my disability in the dust, it was just a Band-Aid solution to a much larger problem. Lies can boost your confidence, they can get you accepted by a group of friends and get you laid, but anything that's not the truth is going to fade.

When I look back at college, I think of people like Emma, who wanted me to believe she was a professional tennis player, and I think of Evan, who was so heavily invested in this idea of being cool that he forgot to be a decent person, and I think of Stephanie, who went from an academic to a cokehead in six months. Most of all, I think of me—denying my disability so I could live what I thought would be a happier life. I can't help but feel so sad for us. We were all under the impression that these reinventions would change us into something better, but they just made everyone more miserable and confused. You can try on different personalities like they're clothing for as long as you want, but I guarantee that the outfit you were originally wearing will always be the one that fits best.

The more distance I have from my college years, the more I realize that it was like a four-year summer camp where your only assignment is to read Judith Butler and feel emotions. I thought it was real, but it was actually just a very expensive dreamworld. And you know what else is a poor imitation of real life? A diet adult world that's meant to give the impression that we're people who are going places. Internships.

The Devil Wears Urban Outfitters

Official Definition of an Internship (According to Dictionary.com)

in·tern·ship, [in-turn-ship] noun

Any official or formal program to provide practical experience for beginners in an occupation or profession

My Definition of an Internship

A period of time in which a twentysomething works for free with no promise of it ever turning into a paid position. Duties include working for someone who is only a year older than you and bringing them coffee, Luna bars, and the occasional Valium. Must know how to photocopy and organize large piles of paper while giving the impression to your boss that you are living the dream!

I first became familiar with the concept of internships from watching *The Hills*—a life-altering reality TV show that followed Lauren Conrad, a beautiful and wealthy high school graduate, as she left behind the sandy cocaine beaches of Laguna Beach for Los Angeles to work a very prestigious internship at *Teen Vogue*. When Lauren found out she got the gig, she acted so excited you would think she had landed a paid position. It was going to be amazing! Her life would never be the same! Move over Diane von Furstenberg. LC's putting on one of her funky headbands and taking over!

When Lauren first came into the *Teen Vogue* offices, the employees prepared her as if she were meeting the pope when she was really just meeting Lisa Love, the West Coast editor in chief. In one truly bizarre scene, they even restyled her outfit so she could look more chic and "*Teen Vogue* appropriate." All this effort proved to be for naught, because Lauren ended up doing jack shit at the magazine. She just sat around a room that looked like a set and gossiped about boys with her fellow intern, Whitney "Just Say No to Having Emotions" Port. Occasionally Lisa Love would make her do something pressing like fly to New York to drop off a dress, but other than that, the whole thing looked like a fake snoozefest. By the end of the series, Lauren had moved on to selling her own cocktail dresses and developing a fashion line for Kohl's while still pretending to live the life of a struggling intern on TV. It was so rude! You can't expect viewers to believe your job is fetching coffee when you're selling a $300 dress called the Audrina.

Even though Lauren Conrad's experience was inauthentic, I was hooked on the idea of interning myself. In the late 2000s, interning had morphed into its own strangely elitist culture, thanks to movies like *The Devil Wears Prada*, which glamorized working for a sadist on a nonexistent salary.

College students everywhere were eager to be abused by some bossy bitch in Isabel Marant because it made us feel accomplished and deluded us into thinking that after putting up with someone's bullshit for an entire summer, we would be guaranteed a job.

This turned out to be laughably untrue. Despite the occasional exception, internships are primarily used by employers to get free labor—especially by the cash-strapped industries I was interested in working in, like publishing. If you do decide to intern (and let's be honest: there isn't much of a choice), you must go into it with no expectations. Just try to get as much experience as you can, make a connection with one of your employers so you can use them as a future reference, and get the fuck out. You are there simply to give your résumé some padding and hope/pray that another company with a bigger budget will be impressed enough to give you an entry-level position.

The summer after my accident, I got my first internship with a website called *Popsense*, which was a tiny pop culture blog run by two twenty-year-old juniors at NYU. I was older than my bosses—a reality that isn't that uncommon in blogging jobs—but I didn't care. I was so desperate to beef up my anorexic résumé I would've picked up dog shit for Suri Cruise. Eugene Lang placed such an importance on internships that I feared I was already falling behind in the rat race. I felt so unaccomplished next to sophomores who would casually rattle off all their internships in class. "Yeah, so I first started interning at sixteen for *Harper's* and then I landed at *McSweeney's* and now I'm at *Vogue*. So I'm, like, on a really good track right now." What the hell? When I was a freshman in college, I was watching *Six Feet Under* in my dorm room with the covers over my head and pretending I had a coke problem. Once, at a party in Los Angeles, I met an intern who was only fourteen years old. I wanted to say to her, "Honey, just go home, pick your zits in the mirror, and call some boys on the telephone. You don't need to do this yet."

But maybe she actually did! The recession hit when I was a junior, and we all scrambled to get any job experience we could before graduating. Since most of my classmates were wealthy to begin with, they could afford to work for no pay for six months. Internships were designed for people like them. They come with an entry fee that rewards the rich and penalizes those who don't have the luxury to work twenty-five hours a week for free while going to school full-time. To work for no money, you must have money to begin with.

Which brings me to my scarlet letter: *m* for malpractice! When I was born a gimp instead of an able-bodied princess, my parents sued my delivery doctor and won me a settlement of money I would receive when I was eighteen. Without this little nest egg, I could have never afforded to live in a city like New York or even intern. Are you kidding? People whose parents file for bankruptcy don't get to intern. That lawsuit was a damn miracle, and I had to take advantage of it. If I just did nothing and got mediocre grades and sat around, I would officially be the worst person ever. (I would also be broke in a few years, because I didn't get *that* much money.)

I ended up working at *Popsense* for a month and a half before I left to have another surgery on my arm. By the time the fall rolled around, I was fully recovered and landed a part-time gig at a more legitimate website, *Flavorwire*. This time I was actually paid ten dollars a post, sometimes twenty if it got a lot of traffic. I was in heaven getting paid to write! I felt so much pride cashing those checks for ten dollars—never mind that each post took me two to three hours to write and format, making the payment less than minimum wage. It felt like I was on the path to success.

In December of 2009, I graduated from college and quit *Flavorwire* to look for a full-time paid writing position, but of course, that didn't work out. New York was still deep-throating the recession and squeezing its balls. There were no jobs for anyone. I was secretly relieved to be unemployed for a little while, though. The prospect of finding work left me paralyzed with fear because I wasn't sure I could even physically survive in the workplace. Wherever I ended up I would have to start from the bottom and do lots of administrative tasks—and with my bum hand and brain, accomplishing something as simple as opening an envelope could take me ten minutes. Trust me, babe. You don't want me to open your mail. Bad things will happen.

To mask my disability to employers, I applied for internships that gave you the option to work remotely. I never once stepped into an office. (Though, to be fair, I think *Popsense* was operated out of someone's dorm room.) I knew I couldn't do this forever, though. If I ever wanted to work in print, or at a legitimate blog, I would need to go into an office and sit side by side with someone. I would have to do simple tasks, tasks that could take an able-bodied person five seconds but possibly hours for me.

I would have to find an internship at a prestigious print magazine.

A few months after I graduated, I was sitting at home watching YouTube videos of Mary-Kate Olsen trying to speak when I saw that one of my favorite magazines, *Interview*, was looking for summer interns. "This is your moment, Ryan!" I thought. "Pick up your confidence that you keep locked in that storage unit in Queens and apply, dammit!" So I did it—I drove to Queens, got my confidence out of storage (it had grown considerably since I'd seen it last, thank God), and applied for the internship. A few days after submitting my résumé, I got a response back asking me to come in for an interview at their intimidating office in SoHo.

Vibrating with excitement, I picked out my best "I am not disabled; I am NEW YORK MEDIA!" outfit and hightailed it downtown to meet with Grace, one of the editors, for a sit-down chat. Grace seemed nice enough, but she did look a bit worn down. It seemed like this job had stolen her spirit and was keeping it hostage in the cat food aisle at Rite Aid. The way she carried herself and the cadence in her voice gave me the impression that the world was perpetually taking a giant dump on her face—a glamorous, couture dump, but a dump nonetheless. Despite her sad vibes, the two of us got along nicely and I felt confident that I had aced the interview.

When Grace called me a few days later and said that I had gotten the internship, I was overjoyed and then immediately terrified. This wasn't a touchy-feely "We understand your brain damage!" magazine. It was an avant-garde New York FASHUN publication that represented physical perfection, and here I was, ready to limp all over it.

It only took thirty minutes into my first day at work to realize that, disabled or not, it was going to be nearly impossible to get a real job at the magazine. Grace was giving me a tour of the office ("This is where you cry after a long day," "This is where you get told you're a retard by your chic power lesbian boss") when, all of a sudden, a flustered assistant came rushing up to her.

"Grace, we need a new magazine rack. The ones we have are falling apart!"

"Are you kidding me?" Grace scoffed. "We can't afford that."

"Um, they're, like, five dollars. I'll just pay for it."

"Okay, fine. You pay."

The assistant slumped away, and Grace continued on with her tour. "This is the Ping-Pong table that no one ever uses because we're not allowed to have fun here . . ." (She wasn't actually saying these things but she might as well have with the way she was delivering the information.) I was shocked. How could this magazine ever afford to hire me if they couldn't even afford a five-dollar magazine rack? Weren't magazines supposed to have money? The office might've been glamorous and the editor in chief was some globe-trotting Anna Wintour–type, but apparently everyone else who worked there was hanging on by a thread—emotionally, spiritually, and financially.

One such person was Hannah, a twenty-four-year-old assistant to the entertainment editor, with whom I worked closely. Since Grace was often crying in a broom closet somewhere, I relied on Hannah to give me things to do. The second I met her, I went into overdrive by sending her pitch after pitch—one of which was a fashion editorial inspired by the Manson family that I don't think went over well. Hannah was sweet, though. She listened to my ideas and encouraged me to scout new music they could possibly feature in the magazine. I did as I was told, flooding her in-box with weird bands that I thought were going to hit it big and creating mini-bios for each group. Hannah took all of these into consideration and immediately got the vibe that I was a hungry tiger. She was calling me by my nickname "Rye" the second day.

It was important to make my presence known at *Interview* so I could set myself apart from the other interns—one of whom I swear to God was South African royalty. That happens a lot at internships. You're always working with someone who's an heiress or whose parents are famous. I have no idea why the wealthy even bother interning in the first place. Maybe they're just looking for ways to kill time before they can marry a wealthy guy named Tad who works in finance and wants to do anal on his birthday.

I was never going to get noticed at *Interview* for my photocopying abilities, so the only other way to make an impression was to showcase my story ideas. This worked in my favor most of the time, until Hannah snapped at me one day and said, "You need to focus less on pitches and fulfill more of your intern duties!" She was absolutely right. I wasn't really doing any of the typical intern work, but that's because I was laughably bad at it. She quickly realized this when, after she ordered me to do the thing I feared most—open mail—I spent thirty minutes trying to work the letter opener and ended up ripping the contents of the envelope.

Sheepishly, I walked up to Hannah, torn envelope in my hand, and apologized for the mistake. She looked annoyed but, sensing the humiliation that was practically radiating from my pores, she took pity on me. "It's okay, Rye," she smiled. "Why don't you go uptown to Bret Easton Ellis's hotel and drop off this manuscript for me?"

Despite all evidence to the contrary, I thought that if Hannah called me by my nickname and gave me positive affirmations, I would somehow get a job. But *nothing* could've gotten me a job at *Interview*. I could've been braiding my boss's hair and married into the family and it still wouldn't have translated to a paycheck. It wasn't anything personal against me. There was just no money to go around. The people who were actually salaried usually ended up doing two jobs for little money. In fact, for the three months I was there, the editorial assistant left to go work at another magazine and instead of immediately hiring someone to fill the position, they had an intern do the job for free. At first, the intern was overjoyed. "Yes!" they thought. "This could be my ticket to getting a real job here." But after months of hard work for no pay, they fired the intern and had someone outside the company fill the position.

As much as I wanted to be offered a job, I left *Interview* disillusioned with the magazine world. Everyone came here to be a part of something they saw on TV, but the reality didn't come close to matching up with the fantasy. The fashion department was especially keen on making their job feel very tortured and glamorous. One day I came into work and an intern rushed up to tell me some "delicious drama."

"Oh my God, you won't believe what happened yesterday!"

"What?"

"A big fashion stylist stopped by the office and went on a rampage. He threw a shoe at an intern's head!" This person seemed positively delighted by this news.

"That's fucked-up."

"I know, right? So nuts!" the intern gushed, smiling.

"No, really. You shouldn't be allowed to treat people that way. I don't care how important you are. That's unacceptable."

"I mean, yeah, I guess. I think it's kind of major, though, to get a shoe thrown at your head by someone that famous."

Excuse me, hon? WHAT THE FUCK IS WRONG WITH MY GENERATION?

On my last day at *Interview*, I had an awkward conversation with Grace and Hannah about my overall job performance that summer. I had finally wised up and was not expecting anything from them. I just wanted to get out of there with my dignity intact. Before I could do that, though, I needed to sit through this conversation of how I was an invaluable part of the team and should really keep in touch. It seemed to me like there was an elephant in the room and that elephant was the fact that I wasn't getting a job. Maybe I was expecting too much, but it did seem strange that it wasn't even being addressed. Finally, I just asked them.

"So, what would I need to do to, like, get a job here?"

Their necks stiffened. It felt like I had just said a curse word: j*b.

"Oh, um . . ." Hannah shuffled uncomfortably in her

Free People peasant top. "You know, we're not really hiring anyone right now, but you should definitely keep in touch with our online editor. You could write more stuff for the site!"

Yeah. *For free.* Everything is for free. With writing, it's an achievement just to be published, which is something I've never understood. Why can't writers expect to get paid, and why is it considered taboo to even bring up the issue of money? In every other industry, you expect payment for your work. You don't have plumbers being like, "YES, I'll unclog your pipes! Thank you for this blessed opportunity. No payment necessary!" Perhaps writers are so willing to work for no money because there's an inherent shame about doing something creative, especially during a time when people are lucky to be working at all. Or maybe we're all just masochists who don't know our own worth.

I had already written for *Interview*'s website and didn't see any point in continuing to work for free. If anything, I would try to diversify as much as possible and try to write somewhere else for no money. I didn't tell Hannah and Grace that, though. I just thanked them for the opportunity and said my good-byes. Before I could leave, Grace told me she had a present for me and led me to her office. She then went underneath her desk and took out a box that was loaded to the brim with children's toys.

"Every intern gets a toy when they leave, and I think I have the perfect one for you!" Grace started rummaging through the box, bypassing Magic Markers and coloring books.

"Oh, here it is!" Grace's face was beaming. She had found the appropriate gift for me: a bright pink Etch A Sketch.

"Wow," I said, genuinely shocked. "I haven't seen one of those in years."

"I know; isn't it funny?"

When I got home, I threw the Etch A Sketch in my closet next to my college diploma, where it belonged. Then I began my months-long stretch of not having a job. Whoever coined the word "funemployment" really needs to lose their job. You don't spend all your time with your friends drinking boxed wine and watching *Keeping Up with the Kardashians*. Your existence is solitary and joyless. You wake up every day feeling immediate dread that you haven't landed something yet. Then you spend hours looking for jobs on the computer. You find yourself applying to anything, things you don't know the first thing about and certainly aren't qualified for, because you're desperate, because you're panicked, because you don't know what else to do. All the while, you have to contend with the fact that just last year, you were living life like it was golden. You were set up for a good future. You did everything right. (If this all sounds naïve and lacking perspective, maybe it's because when you graduate from college, you're naïve and lack perspective.)

Being unemployed is its own full-time job. There's never any true relief. You're always looking for a gig or some unseen opportunity. Meanwhile, there's no escaping the fact that you have no job. It follows you wherever you go. You can't even go on the Internet for a nice distraction, because you'll most likely stumble on some trend piece about how fucked our generation is. The Internet is an overbearing dad wagging his finger in disapproval.

Some of us move back in with our parents. This can light

a fire under your ass and make you start hustling to get a job so you can move out ASAP. Or it can make you sink further into complacency and depression. I have friends who moved back in with their parents after college and just never moved out. A temporary move turned into three years. Just like that. I don't blame them. It's hard to see the world as a land of opportunity from your parents' basement.

I didn't have to move back in with my parents, but that doesn't mean I was living la vida loca when I was unemployed. In fact, I was having a terrible time because I didn't feel like I deserved to experience joy. Every time I let my hair down and cut loose, I'd ask myself, "What have I done to earn this good time? NOTHING! Get a job and then you can have fun. Until then, you're required to be sad."

Being an unemployed postgrad is a modern-day Choose Your Own Adventure. You can be angry and wallow in a sea of entitlement believing that the world has failed you and it owes you something. But don't act surprised when you find yourself not getting what you want. After my accident, I struggled with those pangs of resentment, too. I didn't deserve to get hurt, especially after all I had been through already. When I graduated from college, those familiar feelings resurfaced. I thought, "I'm entitled to a job! I worked hard in school!" But then I realized I sounded like a churlish idiot and shut up and got to work. Getting angry at the world for your problems isn't going to bring you any closer to a dream job or a relationship or whatever else you feel like you deserve. It's going to keep you thousands of miles away from it.

A more effective way you can navigate the unemployed postgrad life is to be fearless. Most people who have achieved a modicum of success right after they graduated did it by being brave and laughing at anyone who told them no. In order to get anywhere, you have to ditch vanity and ego and just say to yourself, "I'm going to look like an idiot for the next few years because I have no idea what I'm doing, but that's okay. That's the only way I'll learn." I've noticed that a lot of my peers have paralyzing self-doubt when it comes to going after the things they want, whether it's a job or a love interest. It makes me think that if you're single, jobless, or both, it's probably because you have a hard time believing you deserve otherwise.

I was having drinks recently with a friend and we were gossiping about an acquaintance of ours who had launched a Kickstarter to film a web series. The premise of the show sounded awful, and the video she made to plead her case was cringeworthy.

"She looks so ridiculous," I snarled. "How could she have done that and thought she looked okay?"

My friend, who is less of a mean gossip girl than I am, said, "You know what? I agree that she looks totally stupid, but I also give her props for putting herself out there. At least she's doing something. Think about all our friends who are unemployed or working at jobs they hate. They talk about all the things they'd like to do, but do they ever end up doing them? No. And that's why people who make embarrassing Kickstarters will probably be more successful than the lazy people who have loads of talent. They're actually doing it, and sometimes that's all you need for things to happen."

My friend was right. A week later, the Kickstarter got funded and our acquaintance quit her job to film the web series. I thought about all the people who, like me, had seen the Kickstarter and immediately sent it to their friends to mock her. They were probably bored at their horrible office job and perked up when they saw a chance to make fun of one of their peers. But who gets the last laugh in that situation? The person who is given the opportunity to do what they love or the insecure jerk who's stuck in a cubicle?

Not giving a fuck about looking stupid is actually the smartest decision you could make, especially when you're establishing yourself after college and have nothing to lose. The only way you can really escape unemployment hell is by taking some risks. Don't be frightened. You can do it, babe! Don't ever forget that Millennials are hustlers. We left school with no clear future and the traditional workplace in pieces, so we had to create our own jobs and build everything from our own intuition. That's one thing twentysomethings don't get enough credit for. The narrative is always "Millennials are bums who live with their parents"—which, fine, that contains an element of truth—but we're also innovative freaks who have a remarkable ability to turn nothing into something.

A year after I graduated from college, I had four internships under my belt and only an Etch A Sketch to show for it. On my twenty-fourth birthday, I was set to start my fifth internship but never ended up going. Instead, I retreated into a writing cave for four months in the hope that something, *anything*, would happen. When I emerged, I had a full-time job and a ticket to a world even scarier than unemployment: the modern workplace.

Young Unprofessional

Ryan, you cannot survive in the real world. Once people figure out that you don't know how to do anything, your days are numbered. You will never be able to hold down a job. Everybody gets it but you.

—Me, on the eve of starting my first job (LOL, bye!)

Is it possible to have a legitimate phobia of having a job? I don't mean like, "Oh my God, I'm too lazy to work. Please let me just lie in bed and listen to sad, fuzzy music forever." I'm talking about a fear of working that leaves you utterly paralyzed. That's what I had. After spending my whole life tricking people into thinking I was more functional than I was, I worried that having a job would undo it all. I had gotten my first taste of having my disabilities exposed when I interned at *Interview*, but the stakes are much lower when you aren't getting paid. Now that I was actually being compensated, I had to prove that I deserved to be there, which is a hard thing to do when you don't exactly believe it yourself. After a few days of working, I was convinced my boss would realize I was an impostor with no real skills and fire me.

If my first job hadn't been so unconventional, perhaps that's what would've happened. When I started my job as a writer and editor at a New York media start-up called *Thought Catalog*, I was the first salaried employee. We had no office and no staff. I worked from home in my pajamas, masturbated to porn on the clock, and spent my lunch break watching TV and eating leftovers from the fridge. I was shocked that a job like this was possible, even though they're not so uncommon anymore. My brother, sister, and I have never worked in an office before. Our jobs all revolve around the Internet and give us the option to work remotely. My parents are mystified by what we do for a living. Professions like "blogger," "porn website creator," and "online curriculum builder" barely existed ten years ago, let alone when they graduated from college. But if the ideal hope for your children is to have them surpass you in success, my parents are getting their wish fulfilled. My brother sold his website at twenty-eight and went into semiretirement the same year my father did. Things like this are possible now. The Internet has enabled people to achieve success quickly. With the traditional pathways muddled, anyone with a Wi-Fi connection and a great idea can rise to the top. There are no rules. We're making it up as we go along.

I'm still not exactly sure how I got a job writing about whatever I wanted at the age of twenty-four, but having money probably helped. The most valuable thing my settlement bought me was the time to write and build a portfolio. If you squint hard enough at people in their twenties who have amazing careers, you'll usually see a trust fund check getting cashed behind them. I don't like to admit it, especially because I didn't grow up with money and it often makes me feel like a traitor to my own class, but it's a fact you can't ignore. I got my dream job because I didn't have to take any nightmare ones.

Being shameless also helped me get to where I wanted to be. Right when I entered the world of unemployment, I started e-mailing every writer and editor in town, asking them how they got to where they were. I sent pitches to anyone who would read them. I wrote every single day, which was a luxury of someone who didn't have to work retail or at a restaurant, and worked on developing my voice until something stuck. Then, after three months of blind panic and working furiously, things began to happen. I started submitting pieces to *Thought Catalog* and they began to receive lots of traffic. By January—my one-year anniversary from my college graduation—I was given a full-time position.

For the first six months of my being employed, I was so euphoric it felt like I was on drugs. (Sometimes I actually was on drugs, but we'll get to my *Requiem for a Dream* moment later.) I wanted to soak everything up and scream nonsense corporate jargon like, "WHERE ARE THE ACTION ITEMS? CAN WE CIRCLE BACK, BOB?" and hand out business cards to everyone I met on the street. Even if it turns out to be dreadful, your first adult job always gives you a perverse thrill. You're thrust into this foreign environment where you have to learn a whole new way of speaking and behaving. It's an exciting electric shock to your system.

One of my duties at *Thought Catalog* involved accompanying my boss to business meetings at bougie artisanal cocktail bars. The person we were getting drinks with would typically be handsome, straight, and young—the type of guy who was groomed for success and had never really spent time being unemployed and freaking out about his future. What was interesting about these business meetings was that nothing would ever get accomplished. You'd spend the first two drinks talking shop and then the cracks would start to appear in the work persona. The timeline of the conversation would typically go like this:

ANATOMY OF AFTER-WORK DRINKS AND NETWORKING

Drink one: You justify why you're here and drinking a $16 cocktail on the company card. You discuss, in vague terms, the possibility of collaboration. You manage to talk for thirty minutes without actually saying anything at all. This skill of talking a lot without speaking definitively is something you learn pretty quickly. Soon, you'll be going to meetings that are about having another meeting. It's very confusing. You may have to lie down in the middle of the conversation and collect yourself.

Drink two: You begin to loosen your necktie and gossip a little bit. "Oh, you know Bob Foreman in accounting? He worked with me at Pelaxaco. Yeah, he's . . . an interesting guy." You then measure your professional dicks to see who's got the biggest one. "You worked at I Am So Blessed Industries for three years? Love that. They offered me a job once but I turned it down to work at I'm More Blessed Industries. That's great that you took it, though. It's an amazing starter job."

Drink three: You make the first mention of having a personal life. You acknowledge, in passing, having a girlfriend or taking a recent vacation to Bermuda. Maybe you talk about where you grew up and make a passing reference to your crazy college days. You're basically saying, "I am drunk enough to admit that I am a nuanced person whose life means more than just having a job." You circle back to your mutual acquaintance, Bob Foreman in accounting, and try to extract some shit-talking. "So listen, I love Bob, would die for him, but the man was an *idiot* when it came to managing a team, wasn't he?" The discussion of Bob's flaws happens slowly, and then it hits like an avalanche.

Drink four: Bob is a fucking asshole. Bob is a life ruiner. Bob gave your friend Cindy genital warts. Also, that job of yours that you bragged so much about during the second drink is actually terrible. Your boss is an insufferable demon, and you make no money. To be honest, you shouldn't collaborate together, because the company won't pay him anything for it. Everything is terrible, ha ha ha!

Drink five: You're fucked. You're ordering a shot. This night is officially turning into a mistake. You're admitting that you're cheating on your girlfriend with someone who likes to stick a finger up your ass. "Where are the hookers? Should we call a hooker?" You're plotting ways in which you can get Bob fired.

Drink six: "I fucking love you, man. You're fucking awesome. Let's start our own fucking company together."

Drink seven: If you're not dead, you're calling your coke dealer.

I love watching someone put on a show, only to slowly settle into the person they really are. What fascinates me about the workplace is this unspoken requirement to adopt a new professional personality, even if everyone knows it's all posturing. You become someone who has never cried over a breakup or thrown up from drinking or failed a class. All the things that make you human are hidden, and you pretend to be someone who always has their shit together. The only place you can really be yourself is happy hour. In college, I thought happy hour was for sad drunk people, but the second I got a job, I was like, "JK; I get it now." If you're working a lot, you only have a small window of opportunity to have fun. From 6:00 p.m. to 9:00 p.m., you can act like it's 3:00 a.m. on a Saturday night and no one will question it. Everyone understands that working full-time can turn you into a borderline alcoholic in five seconds. Not only are you constantly under stress, you're also dealing with insane coworkers all day. Before you had a job, your social life was controlled. Sure, there were crazy people in your classes and sometimes you got stuck talking to a weirdo at a party, but for the most part, you only interacted with people you liked. Jobs are different. Jobs stick a bunch of people with very different personalities in the same room and expect them to learn how to deal with one another. Ordinarily, you'd just be like, "Stop talking to me, you garbage person!" but there's no escaping them in the workplace. You're backed into a cubicle and forced to tolerate those who are fundamentally different from you. It can be a torturous experience, but let's face it: you're going to spend most of your life surrounded by bugaboos, so the quicker you learn how to coexist with them, the better.

Not all coworkers are bad. In fact, sometimes you'll like a coworker so much you will want to fuck them six ways from Sunday. Don't feel guilty about these urges. You're spending more time with this person than your friends and family, so it's only natural that you'd start to be like, "Wait—are you hot? Um, who cares; let's drop this spreadsheet we've been working on and go do forbidden things to each other's bodies." Still, that doesn't mean you should act on it. When you fuck a coworker, you're only fucking yourself, because when things go sour—and they will!—you'll find yourself in a hell of your own making. The only way I would ever advocate coworker sex is if you're convinced that this person is your soul mate, and if that's the case, one of you will have to quit your job in order for the relationship to work. Although it might seem like a major sacrifice, think of it this way: your job isn't going to clean up your vomit when you're sick with the flu or give you an orgasm right when you wake up in the morning.

Thought Catalog was my first big-boy job, and it changed my life overnight. I was immediately ushered into the bizarre world of blogging without an instruction manual. Most of the time I felt like I didn't even work for my boss; I worked for the Internet, which is like the big asshole boss of us all now. The first time I was published online, it was like taking a hit of a powerful drug. The second you post something, you click refresh over and over until you see that someone has left a comment. A wave of adrenaline then washes over you as you keep clicking refresh and watch the responses pile up. The comments run the gamut from "GO KILL YOURSELF" to "This article saved my life!" Then, when the chaos dies down and the chatter begins to dwindle, you come off the high and eventually crash. You start to feel slightly depressed because people have moved on from your article and latched on to something else. At the end of the day, all of the hard work you poured into your piece only ended up amounting to four hours of attention. You think, "What's the point of it all?" until you start to feel the itch for validation again, and the cycle continues.

As a blogger, you face a lot of unconventional problems, but that doesn't mean you're exempt from dealing with typical workplace politics. In every occupation, there's an unspoken rulebook. You can't say certain things about certain people for reasons x, y, and z (the reasons, by the way, are usually bogus and vague, but you aren't allowed to challenge them), and you must be nice to certain powerful figures because they've been deemed important. But since bloggers are so physically alienated from one another, the rules can be even more intense. For example, people have huge fights over something as arbitrary as a work acquaintance deciding not to follow you back on Twitter, or a website is angry with another website for taking its advertisers away, or—oops—someone was made fun of on a blog like *Gawker* by someone they've actually met a few times at parties. Bloggers hope that you'll be too nervous to call them out on their bad behavior in person. They like to pretend the things they do online don't have any effect on the lives they lead outside of work, but everybody knows that's not true. In this day and age, the things we do online almost matter more than the things we do offline.

Beyond having to navigate murky relationships with your professional peers, being a blogger also means you have to deal with the insanity of Internet commenters. One thing I learned very quickly at my job is that people are angry. People are upset about a lot of different things and they take it out on the Internet because it's easy, because it's expected, because the Internet doesn't have a face. I've never understood commenting culture myself. Before working for *Thought Catalog*, I had never once left a comment on a blog post. I just didn't see the point. If I read something I didn't like on the Internet, I would simply x out of it. I never felt a desire to tell someone I didn't know how much their thoughts offended me. I could be doing something far more productive like color coordinating my bookshelves on Adderall. Unfortunately, the Internet attracts this miserable breed of human and provides them with a soapbox on which to stand and TYPE VERY LOUDLY AND ANGRILY. They ruin the fun for everybody. Some days I want to wash the Internet and the gross people who populate it off me, but I guess you can feel frustrated about every job. You work all day and even if you love it, it seeps into your bones and you just want to scrub it from your body: the fluorescent lighting, the sad tuna sandwiches in their Tupperware containers, the phony behavior people adopt to make you respect/fear them, the passive aggressiveness, the competitive mood that looms over the office, the incessant gossiping on Gchat, the burdensome task of trying to look busy when you have nothing to do, the issue of not feeling valued by your employers or, perhaps more accurately, the fear that everyone is going to realize that you've tricked them and you actually have no idea what the hell you're doing. If being in college is all about discovering yourself and embracing your specialness, getting your first real job is about realizing that you know absolutely nothing. It's not a bad thing, though. In fact, it's a gift! Because only when you discover that you know nothing can you really start to learn something.

After spending almost three years of my life being the Internet's slave, I decided I'd had enough. Not only was blogging about my personal life getting monotonous and stale, living in New York was also starting to lose its luster. No one tells you this, but the city is only a fun place to live if you're twenty-one or have twenty-one million dollars. When I first moved there, I was down for anything. "Wow, there's a warehouse party in deep Bushwick starting at one a.m.? Great! I'll just drink some Four Loko and we'll head out!" Even when things didn't turn out the way I wanted them to, I didn't mind, because the pain felt just as exquisite as the euphoria. But, like with every great romance, the honeymoon period had to come to an end. I remember one time taking the subway home after a long day at work and counting down the moments until I could be home in bed watching bad TV. I looked up from the book I was reading and saw an advertisement that said, "You didn't move to New York to stay home." I thought, "Oh my God, you're right. I guess that means I have to leave now." I used to be that person who felt more comfortable being out with my friends than vegging out on the couch, but those days were over. Now I wanted the stuff you couldn't get in New York—like space, quiet, and nice weather. I figured there were 10,000 twenty-three-year-olds who would be more than happy to take my life in New York, so why not let them have it? It's their turn to live in a glorified closet and stay up till 7:00 a.m. and cry on street corners. I was done.

When thinking about where to live next, it took me 1.5 seconds to realize that I should move back to LA. This was for two reasons. One, it was close to my family, and as I got older, I felt a stronger urge to be near them in case they accidentally died a tragic early death. Two, LA was the place I could write my ticket out of the Internet and pursue my dream of being a TV writer. Growing up I was always obsessed with working on television shows. For Christmas and birthdays, I would ask my parents to buy me *Buffy the Vampire Slayer* and *Dawson's Creek* scripts. And whenever I watched something I'd put the closed captioning on so I could pretend I was reading dialogue. In college, I tried my hand at writing fake episodes of shows like *Gossip Girl* with my then BFF Sarah, but then our friendship blew up and I lost the confidence to write without her. I tried to forget about writing for TV and began to make sweet professional love to blogging instead, but the more I wrote for the Internet the more I realized it wasn't a sustainable career path. The pay wasn't great and my ideas were getting recycled over and over for hits. If I had to spend one more minute thinking about what insanely personal aspect of my life had the potential to go viral, I was going to Ctrl+Alt+Delete myself. So before I left New York, I got my shit together and wrote a pilot, which is an episode of an original TV show you use to get staffed on an existing one. My pilot was called *Gimp*, and it's about—what else?—a gay guy with cerebral palsy! I sent it to my book agent, Lydia, who is a boss bitch and just the right amount of terrifying. She read it and was like, "This is hot garbage, Ryan. Go make it better!" Following Lydia's orders, I retreated into my writing cave and emerged a week later with a script that was bearable. Lydia then forwarded it to a talent agency in LA that specialized in TV and film representation. An agent there liked my script enough to take me on as a client, so one month later, I was living in LA and looking for work.

At first I was optimistic about getting a TV job, even though the odds were definitely against me. It's a notoriously difficult business to break into, especially if you are, according to my agent, a "white male with zero connections." Six weeks in, I felt my optimism start to fade as I found myself in the most depressing scenario ever: alone on a Tuesday afternoon in an empty gay bar in Venice Beach nursing a glass of white wine. I had been on my feet all day and needed a place that would let me relax and charge my cell phone without judgment. I had never gone to a gay bar alone before, but it was 3:00 p.m. and the only other people there were two lesbians in cowboy hats, so I figured, "What the hell? This is the perfect place to lose my solo gay bar virginity. Let's hope it doesn't hurt too much!" I sat there, gingerly sipping my white wine, which tasted like delusional dreams, and wondered how the hell I ended up in such professional purgatory. Earlier that day I had talked to my dad on the phone and he asked me, "What happens if you don't get a job writing for TV?"

"It's going to happen, Dad. Trust me."

I told him that not because of ego but because I knew there wasn't any other option for me. If I couldn't write for TV, I'd have to go back to the Internet and do what? Write listicles until I'm eighty? I don't think readers have much of an interest in an article called "10 Signs You Have Dementia." I had to take a gamble on my future to avoid being stuck in a dead-end career, but here I was in LA pursuing my dreams and feeling like an aimless postgrad all over again. You're always one mistake away from being back at the place you were after college: in your underwear, refreshing Craigslist, the heat of your computer searing your thighs. It's the ebb and flow of life. Some days you're on top of the world, sipping champagne and cheering to some professional milestone, and others you're unemployed and alone at a gay bar. Isn't it funny? No. It's not. But it's something.

"Dude," the bearish bartender called out to me. I was near catatonic, staring into my glass of wine, which was starting to look like piss.

"HELLO," the bartender yelled again, loud enough for me to snap out of my fog and register where I was.

"Yeah?"

"Your phone is ringing!" My iPhone had been behind the bar charging. The bartender yanked it out of its charger and threw the phone down in front of me. I saw that it was my agent and remembered he was calling to let me know if I got staffed on an MTV series called *Awkward*. It had been my first staffing meeting ever and I thought it went well, but you never really know. There are a million reasons why you aren't hired on a show, most of which are beyond your control.

I picked up the phone and thought, "Okay. This can either be the darkest moment of my life or the happiest. He might tell me I didn't get the job, and then I'll hang up, cry in public, order ten shots, get wasted, and have a triple kiss with the lesbian cowgirls next to me. Or he might tell me I got it, and then I'll still cry and order ten shots, but I probably won't make the grief-stricken mistake of kissing two lesbian strangers."

"Hello," I answered, my hands shaking on the receiver.

"Hey, Ryan! How are you?" my agent, Tom, asked me.

"I'm at a gay bar by myself, Tom. I've been better."

"Yikes!"

"Yikes indeed. What's up?"

"Well, I just talked to the people over at the network . . ."

I suddenly felt like I was going to vomit. "Oh, really? Awesome. What'd they say?"

Tom paused for a really long time. It was like we were on *The Bachelor* and he was about to tell me if I had been given a rose or not. Agents are so dramatic!

"Ryan . . . you got it!"

I started crying. The bartender and lesbian cowgirls shot me sympathetic looks.

"Are you serious?" I managed to squeak out.

"Yep. You got the job!"

More tears. They never stopped coming. Eventually I had

to tell my agent that I would call him back when I was more stable to get the information. Then I just sat at the bar and continued to cry out of complete and utter happiness.

Your career is comprised of a series of high and low moments. The rejection that comes from pursuing your dreams can be devastating, but it's coupled with these brief instances where you realize you might not be so fucked after all. I'm talking about the times you don't feel like such a hopeless mess and something finally clicks inside you that says, "I can do this!" That's how I felt when I got that phone call. After spending most of my life feeling like an idiot who didn't even know how to break down a box, I figured I was finally onto something. The person who knew nothing was finally starting to learn something.

What We Talk about When We Don't Talk about Money

THERE ARE A LOT of amazing things about writing for television. There's the beauty of collaboration and being able to bounce ideas off some of the most insanely talented and funny people in the world. There's the excitement of watching the words you wrote be brought to life on set by gifted actors. There's the endless supply of snacks, which if you aren't careful, will cause you to gain fifteen pounds in four months. And then there's the money. The money is really good.

Shortly after receiving my first paycheck from working on *Awkward*, I found myself blacked out at a Saks Fifth Avenue in Beverly Hills. I told myself I would only go in to look for a Tom Ford cologne I'd been eyeing (Tuscan Leather, $210), but somewhere along the way, I'd managed to lose my damn mind. After dousing myself in Tuscan Leather, I decided that I wanted—no, *needed*—to add Tom Ford's Tobacco Vanille cologne to my shopping list.

"Hi, hi, hi!" I said manically to the man behind the perfume counter. "Can you come over here for a second?"

"Yes, sir; can I help you?"

"Um, yes," I stuttered. "Do you think it's possible to mix Tobacco Vanille with Tuscan Leather?"

His eyes lit up. "Yes! In fact, those are my two favorite colognes to mix. This is the Tom Ford Private Blend collection, which means that they're actually meant to be combined with other scents."

"Wow!" I swooned, wiping some sweat away from my forehead. "I could tell that Tuscan Leather wasn't necessarily a stand-alone scent. What other colognes do people mix it with?"

"Sandalwood is very popular." The man sprayed some Sandalwood on my wrist, and my whole body convulsed in ecstasy. Suddenly I was convinced that I was only three $210 bottles of cologne away from being the person I was meant to be.

"That smells amazing! I've been on the hunt for a scent that feels the most like me, but to be honest, I don't think I found it until today."

"I understand completely. People spend years searching for something that best fits their personality. It's not easy." The perfume guy eyed me slowly. "I can tell by your personality that Sandalwood, Tuscan Leather, and Tobacco Vanille are three scents that accurately represent you. They're sexy and mysterious."

"You really think so? Thanks so much." I smiled coyly. Even though I knew this guy had no interest in seeing me naked, I appreciated him going the extra mile for his commission.

"So, what are we thinking? Do you want to get them?"

My body was buzzing. My armpits were dripping sweat. I felt high out of my mind and so alive.

"Let's do it."

He swiped my credit card, and I felt a surge of pleasure go through my entire body. I took my three tiny bags and ran toward the exit, thinking to myself, "Ryan, you need to get out of here. Things are about to get dangerous!" Then I saw a beautiful display of candles out of the corner of my eye and knew that I was dead. Candles are my favorite things in the world. Sometimes I have fantasies of loading them up in a baby stroller like they're my children and taking them on a scenic walk. When I'm around them, I'm powerless.

Two hours later, I emerged from Saks Fifth Avenue with three colognes, six Diptyque candles, and a tiny jar of La Mer eye wrinkle cream ($285). Now that the spending spree was over, the adrenaline had faded and I was left feeling utterly depleted. It cruelly dawned on me that I had spent almost my entire paycheck in an afternoon.

When I want to spend money, nothing can stop me. It's the same feeling you get when you're horny. The craving comes over you and dominates your brain until you find a way to quench it. You immediately enter a fugue state where beautiful objects replace logic. At a certain point, your standards will lower and it won't even matter what you get. You just need to experience some instant gratification as quickly as possible. Swiping your credit card and leaving a store with a bunch of shopping bags is not dissimilar to coming all over someone's chest. Both are a release. But once the euphoria fades, you come to your senses and assess the damage. In the case of getting laid, it might be realizing that the stranger you picked up at a bar looked a whole lot cuter to you an orgasm ago. With spending money, it's processing the fact that you spent almost $300 in twenty minutes and now have an $80 candle that doesn't even smell that great.

I don't go shopping very often, but when I do, events like the Saks Fifth Avenue Massacre happen. None of the things I buy make sense to me at first (lemonade mix from a high-end furniture store and $30 hand soap?), but then I realize they're all things I think the better version of me should have. I buy stuff so people can see it and think, "Wow, who is that guy with an extensive candle collection and fresh-cut flowers on the dining table? He's so together!" Whether you have money or not, the point of being a consumer in your twenties seems to be less about making yourself happy in the moment and more about taking the necessary steps toward becoming the person you want to be.

People don't like to talk about these kinds of things. If you ever want to clear a room, just bring up the subject of money. Walk up to someone and ask, "How can you afford to live?" Chances are the person will scream bloody murder, tear out clumps of their hair, and run out of the emergency exit before they answer that question. Money is not something we're supposed to discuss. Or if we do talk about it, it should always be in the context of us not having any. When someone tells you that they like your top and it happens to be inexpensive, you say, "Twenty dollars at H&M. Can you believe it?" But if someone compliments you on something you bought at Marc Jacobs for $200, you're embarrassed and say "Thanks" instead.

I get why people are uncomfortable talking about their finances. Money is tricky—especially in your twenties—because it so clearly separates the people who were born with it from those who've yet to make it on their own. In one group, you have the privileged few who are either supported completely by their parents or at least get a little bit of help each month. For some, this affluence can be a major source of shame because rich kids don't like being different. They want to "rough it" along with their peers and be able to say, "OMG, I'm broke too!" Sometimes they'll go so far as to pretend they're struggling anyway, which is so insulting. Once a very rich friend of mine was complaining about how she couldn't afford groceries. The next day she showed up to lunch with a new Miu Miu bag. In college, I knew a rich kid who lived in a doorman building and moonlighted as a dishwasher because he said it felt like honest work. What is with rich people's FOMO about being broke? It's not fun!

Then you have those who are working toward some semblance of financial security. They look at apartments, they look at lattes, they look at cashmere sweaters, and all they see is a price tag, something that could catapult their entire existence into debt and misery. Money is the enemy. When they look around, all they see is people who have it better than they do, people with tans from their exotic vacations wearing expensive makeup and jewelry they bought with their "fuck you" money. In a city like New York, where I spent most of my twenties, the concept of wealth is completely distorted. You could come from the richest family in Kentucky, but when you move to the city, you feel destitute. True poverty exists here, just like it does everywhere else in the world, but the people who often identify as being poor in the city are usually, in fact, not poor at all. They're just living in New York.

I've always been obsessed with rich people who have a tenuous grasp on reality. Luckily for me, delusional trustafarians seem to be everywhere these days. They're at your dry cleaner getting their designer dresses tailored or standing in the corner of a grungy house party plotting to steal your boyfriend. The rich often live among us in disguise so as not to give their class away, but don't be fooled by their ratty flannels and scuffed boots. That outfit costs $3,000. The stains on their faded jeans? Those were imported from France, you plebeian.

Here's how you can tell if someone is rich. Number one: they live in Manhattan, Paris, San Francisco, or any other swinging metropolitan city. I know *rich* is a relative term, but if you can afford to pay sky-high rents, you're already richer than most third world countries. Secondly, you have to understand that the rich have their own language, especially when speaking to each other. They say strange things like, "My parents bought me this apartment as an investment . . ." which, okay, yes—I get it. Real estate is certainly a wise investment, but you do realize that makes you a twentysomething homeowner, right? You know what's considered a good investment at the age of twenty-four? Condoms. A nice pair of winter boots. Not lucrative property.

Rich people also like to say things like, "I left that at my summer house," "My horse is acting out!" and "Dubai is actually kind of cool, you guys . . ." Someone who is well traveled is usually wealthy. Name a country in front of them and they'll be like, "OMG, I love [insert weird place here]. If you go, you have to visit this *amazing* restaurant on the river that serves the best chimichangas. Ask for Mambo! He's an old family friend!" The old family friend is another important signifier of class. Rich families like to travel in packs so that wherever they go they have a filial connection, a place to crash, and a job waiting for them. They look out for their own. Meanwhile, the only place I have connections is Costco, where my dad is considered to be a very important customer.

Other ways to tell if someone is rich: they have nice shampoo, conditioner, and face cream. Rich people don't like to be too grandiose anymore, so most of their money goes into the small details. Visit a rich person's bathroom and all their secrets will be revealed to you. Their couch may say recession, but their medicine cabinet is still living high on the hog. Lastly, someone is rich if they have a name like Scoop, Muffy, Mitsy, or Scooter. The more made-up a name is, the richer they are. Nothing says "I DON'T GIVE A FUCK BECAUSE I'M RICH, BITCH!" like naming your daughter Acorn.

Even though I technically grew up middle class, I've been around rich people since I attended St. Paul's on financial aid. While all the other mothers dropped their kids off at school wearing their tennis outfits and stopped in the parking lot afterward to leisurely chat and gossip, mine was always like,

"Get the fuck out of the car, sweetie. If I'm late to work, I get fired and we lose everything!"

My family did have occasional glimmers of wealth. For a few years, we lived in a nice house in the hills, and at one point my father even owned a BMW (which he later couldn't afford, so he traded it in for a piece-of-shit Buick that eventually broke down in a Taco Bell drive-thru). But as soon as we'd start to feel cozy, as soon as things would get comfortable, we'd lose it all. When my parents divorced and filed for bankruptcy, my mother had to buy a much smaller house in a less desirable part of town. My father moved into a two-bedroom apartment where I took up residence in the walk-in closet. (To this day, my father doesn't think it was weird for his son to live in a closet and insists it was the size of a small bedroom. It wasn't. It was the size of a closet.) My father was offensively cheap. Whenever we would grab burgers at a fast-food restaurant for dinner, he would refuse to do something as simple as pay the extra sixty cents for cheese, insisting that he could melt cheese in a pan himself when we got home. We could also never order anything other than water when we were at a restaurant. Suggesting that you'd like to have a Sprite was basically like demanding that he send you to Sarah Lawrence for college. Whenever I asked him why he wouldn't buy me a soda, he would say, "BECAUSE IT OFFENDS ME THAT THEY'RE EVEN CHARGING FOR SOFT DRINKS. IT'S THE PRINCIPLE OF THE MATTER, RYAN!"

As I got older, my father remained cheap as ever, but somehow he, my brother, and I all managed to move up in class. When I was fourteen, my father remarried a sitcom writer and moved into her beach house in Malibu. When I was eighteen, I got access to my settlement money, and my parents were basically like "K, bye—no more money for you." (One of the first things I did with my money was take my dad out to dinner and order a million Sprites just to spite him. It was a bittersweet moment because no purchase has ever felt as gratifying since.) After I received my lump sum of cash, my brother started his very successful porn website and bought a million-dollar house in the Hollywood Hills. Soon, the three of us were eating out at steakhouses and experiencing a lifestyle that was wildly different from the one we grew up with. We had reached financial stability thanks to second marriages, porn, and cerebral palsy.

I'll never forget the day I got my settlement money. On my eighteenth birthday, I went into a Washington Mutual (RIP) and took out $300, which was the most amount of money I'd ever seen in my life. Holding those crisp $20 bills in my hand felt like being in possession of crack cocaine. I just wanted to use it until there was nothing left. So that's what I did. I had Baby's First Spending Blackout in the mall. I bought a few CDs at Sam Goody, an ice blended mocha at Coffee Bean & Tea Leaf, a new wallet at the skater shop, and some T-shirts at Miller's Outpost. I bought lemonades for all my friends at Hot Dog on a Stick and took a cab downtown to go to the movies. I was an instant nouveau riche teen nightmare. Growing up in a household that was dominated by financial stress, I'd never thought of money as a happy thing. It was the source of depression, anxiety, and fear—not a cause for celebration.

It felt strange gaining access to a world that was never

meant for me. The switch reminded me of my car accident, when I had gone from being Ryan, the dude with cerebral palsy, to Ryan, the poor guy who got hit by a car. I was again wearing the personality clothes that didn't quite fit. People assumed I came from a wealthy family and had a trust fund when it couldn't have been further from the truth. Cerebral palsy, the source of all my major issues and internal strife, was the reason why I was able to order an $18 salad at [insert hot restaurant here].

Having money meant I dodged a crucial aspect of your twenties: being broke. In college and beyond, you're supposed to have a hard time financially. If you don't, it's a strike against your character. Many of my friends take pride in their working-class roots and have told me that they wouldn't date someone who's rich because the class inequity would make them too uncomfortable. Once, a friend of mine who'd ended up with a wealthy boyfriend accompanied him and his family on a shopping trip to SoHo and watched them drop thousands of dollars in two hours. Afterward, she was so traumatized that she had to excuse herself to go cry in the bathroom. I don't blame her. Money is depressing. Gallivanting around with rich people when you yourself don't have much money can lead to secretly sobbing in bathrooms because you're being faced with the cold, harsh reality that no matter how alike you are, there are always different upbringings, different reference points, different values placed on the dollar.

Most of my friends were raised in middle-class households and no longer receive any help from their parents. At least I don't think they do. Getting a postgrad to talk candidly about their financial situation isn't easy. I think I'd have a better chance getting one of my girlfriends to share the story of her second abortion. It seemed like whenever I tried to talk to one of my friends about how they get their money, the conversation would go like this:

Me: Hey, babe!
Friend: Hey, hon! What's up?
Me: Nothing. I was just wondering if I could ask you some questions.
Friend: Sure. What about?
Me: Um, I want to know how you afford to live.
[DIAL TONE]

Perhaps people are so reticent to talk about money not because they all have a secret trust fund but because they're ashamed of their spending habits. No matter how "broke" a twentysomething claims to be, they will always be able to afford the things they "need"—even if that thing is something as superfluous as a bottle of wine or an organic five-dollar latte.

It goes back to the reason why I blow all my money on candles, lotions, and potions. In your twenties, you are constantly aspiring to be *something*—a girlfriend, a young professional, someone with health insurance, a person who knows how to cook—and in order to get from point A to point B, you feel like you have to drop some serious cash. Take the simple desire of wanting to get laid. To feel sexually attractive, one believes they have to work out at the gym, buy clothes that make their body look amazing, and spend extra money on healthy locally sustainable, hormone-free, very expensive food. So they do it. They go to Whole Foods, they buy a gym membership at a place like 24 Hour Fitness, which is cheaper than, say, Equinox, but is still a lot of money for someone who considers themselves broke, and they splurge on the occasional shopping trip to Forever 21 and H&M. This is what "living paycheck to paycheck" looks like for a lot of people: delicious groceries, a lot of throwaway dresses, and maintaining a gym body. They're seen as necessities instead of luxuries, though, because Millennials need to look good and feel good, no matter what their paycheck says.

To get further insight into the troubled delusional minds of my generation, I've compiled a list of the top ten things "broke" twentysomethings buy and the rationale behind each purchase:

1. *Alcohol:* I need to buy this orange hibiscus cocktail because I'm sad and I'm sad because I don't have any money and I don't have any money because I keep spending all my money on orange hibiscus cocktails.
2. *Cabs:* It's late and I don't want to walk home because I'm scared of getting raped. Do you want me to get raped?
3. *Dinners at expensive restaurants:* My friend suggested this place and I feel too embarrassed to tell her that I can't afford it, so I said yes and now I'm having heart palpitations. I better not get too nervous and vomit up this $24 chicken breast I charged on my credit card.
4. *New sheets:* My old sheets were only 250-thread count, which just isn't okay because I'm twenty-six now and twenty-six-year-olds deserve a higher thread count.

5. *The expensive organic cereal:* I need to eat healthy, okay? I haven't been taking care of myself lately, so I'm investing in this organic cereal in the hopes that it will minimize the damage alcohol has wrought on my body for the last five years. Besides, it's only $6.
6. *Student loans:* This isn't actually a superfluous purchase, but LOL at people who are like, "I'm deferring my loans because I have no money. Can we talk about this later, though? I'm late to yoga."
7. *Nice jeans:* Um, they last forever, and anyway it's smart to invest in classics like a good pair of jeans and shoes. Plus, they make my ass look amazing, so bye!
8. *iPhones:* If a homeless person can have an iPhone, so can I!
9. *New computer:* My computer is so slow that I can't even check for jobs on Craigslist. You want me to be employed, right?
10. *Cable:* JK—who actually has cable anymore?

All my friends are in such different places financially. I know people who are still living with their parents in my hometown because they can't afford rent, people whose parents pay for their $3,000-a-month studio in Manhattan, people who make $45K a year and support themselves completely. I even know someone who is homeless and has been crashing with friends in Los Angeles for the past year doing the occasional odd job. The idea of "struggle" is completely relative, and even though I'm friends with everyone from trust funders to people who don't have a place to live, they all seem to be doing okay. They all manage to make it work and live lifestyles that aren't so night and day from one another. Sometimes I wonder how this could be possible. Does this mean that everyone I know is just living beyond their means and spiraling into credit card debt? No. It means we're operating under the assumption that everything is going to work out. We have a crystal clear vision of what our life is supposed to look like. We will be able to go on vacations. We will be able to afford nice bath products. We will be able to go out to a nice dinner. And we will work our ass off and do whatever it takes to make sure that happens. If for some sick, strange reason it doesn't work out, our financial bottom isn't really a bottom at all. We can just move back in with our parents until we land on our feet again. In previous generations, you had legitimate pressure to get your shit together, because there was no bailout plan. Millennials are different. Whether you're rich or poor, most of us have the safety net of our parents' house, and that allows us to live the life we want. That's our secret. It's not credit card debt. It's not trust funds. It's having parents who don't want to see us fail.

My mom would love nothing more than for me to move back into her house and live unhappily ever after, but that would only happen if hell freezes over and/or Vanessa Hudgens is considered a legitimate actress. Even if I did manage to blow through all my money and my TV career turned to dust, I'd still never go back to sharing a roof with my parents. My days of being a closeted teenager who lives in an actual closet are over.

Being Gay Is Gay

BEHIND EVERY SUCCESSFUL TWENTYSOMETHING gay man, there is an ashamed thirteen-year-old boy jacking off to Mark Wahlberg under the covers. I remember the moment I realized I was gay. It wasn't when, at the tender age of seven, I wore a T-shirt around my head and pranced around the house pretending I had long luxurious blond hair à la Kelly Taylor in *Beverly Hills, 90210.* Nor was it when I noticed that my best friend in the third grade, Todd, had a remarkably cute butt and would stare at it for hours in class. All of that seemed like normal behavior to me. What guy didn't pretend to have long hair and check out his best friend's ass when he was younger? Okay, maybe there were a few.

My first inkling that I might be just a smidge homo came when puberty hit and I began to spend approximately 80 percent of my waking hours in the shower masturbating. At first I would fantasize about men and women, convincing myself that I was only thinking about dudes for logistical sex reasons, but after two weeks of engaging in that heterosexual nonsense, my brain started to slip up and kick the girl out of the fantasy. Now that I was faced with only an image of hot, hunky male parts, all pleasurable hell would break loose in my body.

"You've got to be kidding me," I screamed to myself in the shower, shortly after climaxing to my first male-only fantasy. This couldn't be happening. I did *not* want to be gay. Not because I thought my parents and friends would disapprove—no; I knew they wouldn't care, thank God. I was pissed because the chances of an average-looking gay guy with cerebral palsy having a fruitful sex life seemed slimmer than a thirty-inch waist. Gay men are superficial. Well, everyone is superficial, but for some reason gay men are allowed to embrace their judgmental behavior and take pride in their elitism. How could a gay like me ever make a splash when hot able-bodied guys were getting denied?

I spent most of my adolescence in the closet, hoping that one day I'd find the urge to jack off to Buffy and all would be right again. That day, of course, never came. But *I* still did! I came all over the place. In my usual favorite spot, the shower, in the living room when I was home alone and watching *Queer as Folk*, which I had explained to my mom that I only watched for the captivating storylines, and in my room, which, as I mentioned before, was an actual closet. The benefit of spending all your time in a literal and figurative closet is that you become an expert at hiding your sexuality. You learn your way around anonymous Internet browsers that will let you look at gay porn on your family computer without leaving a trace and feign disgust when your best girlfriends talk about men. It's a part that every gay man was born to play, at least for a little while. I lasted until I was seventeen, and then I couldn't take it anymore. At the end of my junior year of high school, it dawned on me that telling my friends I had a serious crush on Parker Posey wasn't cutting it. I needed to finally come out and taste the rainbow.

Instead of breaking the news slowly, however, I decided to tell everyone I knew by throwing myself a giant coming-out party. I sent out a mass text that said, "MOM IS OUT OF TOWN, SO YOU KNOW WHAT THAT MEANS! PARTY AT MY HOUSE SATURDAY! OH BTW, I HAVE A GIANT SECRET TO TELL ALL OF YOU. IT'S A BIG DEAL AND WILL CHANGE ALL OF OUR LIVES FOREVER. SEE YOU THERE!" My friends arrived at my house wondering what this big secret could possibly be. Did it involve the gift bags full of penis pasta and sex toys that were sitting on my kitchen table?

"Hey, guys," I greeted everybody while wearing a hideous rainbow stripe shirt I had bought specifically for the occasion. "Sit down. I have something I'd like to show you."

Earlier that day, I came out to my best friend, Caitie, and we filmed a little video for the big reveal. It opened with the two of us slow dancing in my room. The mood was romantic—candles were lit, and soft jazz was floating from the stereo. All of a sudden, Caitie started to close in on a kiss and my body recoiled.

"What's wrong?" Caitie cried out.

"I can't do this," I sighed dramatically. "I wish I could, but . . . I just can't!"

Caitie took me over to my bed, sat me down, and placed a reassuring hand on my knee. "My sweet rose, just tell me what's wrong."

"I'm afraid this secret is too sinful to ever divulge!"

"You can trust me, honey . . ."

I let out an exasperated sigh. "Okay, fine. You asked for the truth, and I'm going to give it to you!"

The lens zoomed in on my face, and I looked up at the camera. After a pregnant pause, I finally screamed out, "I'M GAY, BITCHES!"

All my friends immediately cheered and enveloped me in a group hug. I couldn't believe how perfect it had all come together. Not only did people not care I was gay, but they were obsessed. When I told my mom and dad a few days later, they were both like, "That's cute. What do you want for dinner?"

Now that I had everybody's love and acceptance, my next order of business was to touch a penis. I'm what you call a gold-star gay—someone who has never bothered to take a dip in the pussy pond—so you can imagine how, at seventeen, I was salivating at the opportunity to hook up with someone. Unfortunately, my small town wasn't exactly swimming with out-and-proud teenagers. It was just me and a sophomore named Julio who had severe cystic acne and liked to dance to Gwen Stefani at lunch.

Desperate, I called up one of my long-lost childhood buddies, Dan, who I had always suspected was a big 'mo, and said, "Hi, I'm gay now, so do you want to come over and hook up?" Despite swearing he wasn't gay himself, he agreed to come to my house the next day to fool around. You know, because he was such a good friend.

When Dan arrived, I took his hand and led him to my room. It was in the middle of the afternoon and the sun was still peeking through the curtains. There was no Sade playing in the background or a dark night to hide our bodies. Years later, after having so many wasted hookups at 4:00 a.m. with a playlist blaring from my iPod, I realize now that my first hookup was actually pretty intimate. There were no excuses to make. No alcohol to place the blame on. I was, for the first time, being completely honest with myself about what I wanted.

Dan and I started kissing on the bed. After a few moments, he had to stop and show me how to make out with someone without mistaking their mouth for a jar of Nutella. Once the kissing tutorial was done, I pulled down his underwear and found a dick so huge it would make Ron Jeremy's dick enroll in a self-esteem workshop.

"Your dick is, um, very large, Dan. Are you aware of this?"

Dan looked down at it with casual indifference. "I mean, I guess. It's not that big."

"Nope—it's big. I don't know dick very well, but I do know that this one means business."

He shrugged. "Okay. Sweet."

I studied it carefully like it was cafeteria mystery meat. I wanted to wrap it around my wrist like a watch or, at the very least, poke at it a little bit. Instead, I did what every normal Bicurious George would do: I went down on it.

Giving your first blow job is terrifying, but giving it to a dick that is only meant for advanced users is a legit nightmare. I didn't know what my gag reflexes were. I didn't even know how to purse my lips to avoid an unfortunate teeth situation. Thankfully, teenage boys aren't the harshest critics when it comes to getting head. Most of the time they just feel so blessed to have a mouth on their penis that they're going to keep quiet. They won't stop you in the middle of it and be like, "You know what? Before you go any further, I have some notes I'd like to give you."

After going down on Dan for some time, I was starting to get painful lockjaw. He was taking forever to come. I'm sure as soon as he was starting to get somewhere, I would accidentally take a bite out of his penis and send him right back to square one. I finally just threw up my hands in defeat and decided to give him a hand job instead.

Big mistake. Hand jobs are everyone's least favorite thing to do on the sexual activity tree. I don't know a single person who's like, "Oh my God, you know what I just love to do to a guy? I love to spit on my hand and then rub it on their dick awkwardly for about ten minutes. I'm, like, really good at it." Hand jobs are designed to make us feel bad about ourselves. I've been fired from a lot of them, including the first one I gave Dan. (Well, technically, I quit.) It took me only six jerks to realize that this was not going to be my sexual journey, so I stopped and politely suggested that we jack ourselves off. Dan agreed, and ten seconds later, we both came in unison. It was super cute.

The second I climaxed and exited the sexual fog, I told Dan that he needed to get going. It wasn't because I was ashamed of what I had just done. On the contrary, I was overjoyed. I got my first kiss, my first hand job, and my first blow job out of the way in a single day. Talk about killing three birds with one very sexually frustrated stone. I just had no feelings for him. I had hooked up with someone who was essentially a gateway gay, someone who could carry me over to better prospects. There were no real emotions involved. Plus, there was no way I was going to have my first anal sex experience with a dick that massive.

Instead of focusing on boys, I decided to spend the next few months riding the natural high you get from living your life the way you want for the first time ever. But then something took me by surprise. I fell in love with a boy. When I saw Charlie, a beautiful Latin dude with huge lips, from across my school quad, I thought, "This guy is going to change my life." I introduced myself to him. He was wearing a Smiths T-shirt that had been cut into a muscle tee, and he looked like something out of a blissful gay fantasy.

"I love your shirt," I said. "What's your favorite Smiths song?"

"Thanks! 'Frankly, Mr. Shankly' for sure."

"Oh my God—me too!" I lied. It was really "That Joke Isn't Funny Anymore," but whatever. I would've told him that I liked Nickelback if it meant that he would be into me.

I knew Charlie was gay. Not because of what he was wearing—although a Smiths T-shirt didn't hurt—but because I felt it. It's an indescribable feeling, one you get when you're young and grow up in a town with people who don't look at things the same way you do. I had come out of the closet to much fanfare, but it really only solved half my problem. I still hadn't found someone to be part of my gay tribe. That's why, when I met Charlie, it was as if I was seeing everything clear and queer for the first time. He was the peanut butter to my jelly, the one who was going to make me feel like less of a weirdo.

After we parted ways, my whole body was vibrating. It felt like I was high out of my mind, and in a way, I was. The most powerful high is the one you get when you're a teenager who's about to fall in love. There's nothing quite like it.

Charlie and I became attached at the platonic dick. We had sleepovers at each other's houses, drove to LA to go to concerts, and had bonfires on the beach. The benefit of Charlie being closeted to his family was that I could share a bed with him without his parents worrying we were hooking up. When summer started, it wasn't uncommon for Charlie and me to spend three days together just walking all over our town, talking for hours. That's the thing that's always baffled me about being young. Your life is so boring and yet you never run out of things to talk about.

Charlie and I had been friends for only a few weeks when he told me he was gay. A few of his friends knew, but to everyone else he was closeted. "I still plan on marrying a woman and having a white picket fence and all that," he told me in my room. It was in the middle of the day, around the same time Dan and I had hooked up a month earlier. "We'll see if that happens."

Spoiler: it never happened. As Charlie and I got closer, all our interactions became more and more sexually charged. Finally, one day on AIM, Charlie asked me if I'd like to be his boyfriend. My stomach went into a free fall. Here was someone who was beautiful, warm, and funny, and he wanted me? Unclear.

What followed after that felt like some coming-of-age gay teen movie you'd rent On Demand. Charlie and I spent every moment together, mostly in my bed getting to know each other's bodies. We were like two scientists poking around each other and being like, "Okay, what happens when I do this to you?" I told myself I'd wait until Charlie and I were like *really* in love to have gay sex, which, in teenager time, only took about two weeks.

There was one issue with losing my virginity, though: I didn't know a single thing about anal sex. My private Episcopalian school left that section out during sex ed. So I went to my local Barnes & Noble and bought a book called *Anal Pleasure and Health* and read all the chapters, studied the illustrated pictures, and took notes.

"Charlie, you have to read this book I just bought. It's all about anal!" I squealed.

Charlie looked at the book and made a sour face. "Babe, I think you've been watching too much *Sex and the City*. Can't we just try it and take it from there?"

I couldn't argue with that. Ten minutes later, I found myself flat on my stomach and ready to go. (We tried having my legs up in the air but, um, it didn't really work. Cerebral palsy problems!)

"Okay, tell me when it's going in," I said.

"Of course."

A few seconds passed before I screamed out in pain. "Charlie, I told you to tell me when you were going in!"

"Ryan, I literally just grazed you with my dick."

"Oh. Fuck. Well then, slower, please."

"Okay, babe." Charlie started again with trepidation and went in very delicately. "Is that okay?"

"Sure," I squeaked. The truth was that it felt like a bowling ball just entered my asshole. Having a dick in your ass, even when it feels amazing and your prostate is doing a happy dance, feels strange. There's no way around it. The whole thing just feels so unnatural, which is partially why anal sex feels so hot. When you're letting a dude fuck you, you immediately feel close to him because it's such an intense act. I mean, you're letting someone go inside your butt. Sometimes it feels like they're going so far inside that their dick is going to pop out of your stomach like that little baby in *Alien*! It's that crazy. And if you're like me and don't do anal that often, your asshole is probably tighter than the door at Studio 54. Tight assholes are beneficial for the person who's giving but not for the dude who's receiving.

So here we were—Charlie was putting his hot dog through my keyhole and I was actually starting to like it. I was still lying on my stomach in pain, but I was beginning to experience these flashes of pleasure I'd never had before. It's hard to even articulate what this kind of pleasure feels like. There's a lot of involuntary moaning. I'll just be getting fucked when all of a sudden my mouth will start to contort and this whimpering, animalistic sound will escape my lips. Afterward, I'm like, "How did that sound come out of my body without any warning? That was cool!"

I was getting the hang of this whole anal sex thing. After thirty minutes of Charlie fucking me, I went from feeling weird and vulnerable to being a full-fledged lesbian who wanted to shout out Ani DiFranco lyrics during sex. With every thrust, I was thinking, "Okay, so we're definitely going to get married, but where? Maybe on a vineyard in Napa or on the beach in Provincetown, although I would hate to make both of our families travel that far. And after the wedding, we're going to hire a surrogate to have our biracial babies. One will be named Donovan, and he'll play the clarinet. Let's pray he's gay like his daddies!"

But just as I was about to scream, "Oh my God, you're the best. Just put a ring on it!" I smelled something weird, something funky, something you should never smell during sex.

"Charlie, do you smell that?" I asked, turning slightly to see him pounding into me, drenched in sweat.

"What?" he panted. "No."

"Okay . . ." I continued to lie there on my stomach and pretend that what I feared was happening was actually just a figment of my imagination. But then time passed and the stench grew. It was getting to be undeniable. I was smelling the scent of my shit on Charlie's dick.

No one really talks about how common it is for a little shit to come out of your ass during anal sex. This is, after all, why gay men do enemas and colonics. I didn't know this then, though. I thought I was the first person in history to poop on their boyfriend.

"Charlie, stop! I think I'm pooping!"

Charlie, who had a front-row seat to the production of my asshole, already knew what was going on and didn't care.

"I'm almost there," he told me. "Don't worry. Just hold on!"

"No, please!" I begged. "Let's stop. I'm freaking out!"

"It's not a big deal. Just wait a sec."

After an agonizing two minutes passed, Charlie finally came and I pushed him off me to run to the bathroom. So much for a tender postcoital embrace. I had shit I needed to clean off my body. People often look in the mirror after they have sex for the first time to see if they look different, and in my case, I actually did. I had an expression of pure panic on my face that I had never seen before and shit smears on my leg. Charlie remained cool throughout the whole thing, which was as much of a blessing as it was disconcerting. The next day, I Googled "anal sex poop" and learned I wasn't a freak with irritable bowel syndrome. People have been pooping on their partners during anal since the dawn of time. Phew. Good to know.

Despite getting off to an, um, shitty start, Charlie and I continued to have sex more or less without incident. It was nice. It was special. It was, at times, almost too intense. And sex would never really feel that way again. This is not a good or a bad thing. It just is.

Right before I left for college in San Francisco, Charlie and I broke up. As sad as I was to be single again, I left my small town thinking I was about to be up to my chest in dick. If I could get laid in sad heterosexual Republican Ventura, imagine the possibilities that awaited me in the swinging liberal city of SF!

It turns out that the only thing that was waiting for me at college was a ten-pound weight gain and a long stretch of celibacy. I lived in San Francisco for two years and didn't so much as kiss a boy. You know how they say that being gay gets better? Well, when you come out and get the complete acceptance of your family and friends, throw yourself a killer party, and fall in love all in less than a year, being gay can only get worse. Much worse.

It gets worse when you sift through gay personal ads and find that most guys are only into "straight-acting men," which loosely translates to, "I don't want to date a femme queen." Oh, the misogyny of it all! To the boys who don't want their lovers to act girly, I suggest you just spend your time getting frat boys drunk and fondling them. That's what you really want, right? A big guy named Bob who will ignore you after you give him a blow job?

It gets worse when you're expected to have a vested interest in the lives and careers of Beyoncé and Lady Gaga. Bombshell: I don't really listen to either of those ladies. I'll put some "Drunk in Love" on when I'm blotto and want to turn the mother out, but I'm more interested in listening to music that makes me want to kill myself. It's a personal preference. Just because I was born with dick loving in my genes doesn't mean my body starts to involuntarily move at the sound of a dance beat.

It gets worse if you're fat, ugly, or short. Actually, JK on the short part, because it seems like 75 percent of the gay population is 5′6″ or below. What's up with that, anyway? Are they making gay people smaller these days? They would.

It gets worse if you want a long-term monogamous relationship. Here's the line of thinking most gay men have about relationships: "Damn it, I want a boyfriend. I hate being single! I just want to move in with a sweet dude and get a dog and be that gay couple who throws dinner parties and shit. Oh, wait—I can't because I'm scared of intimacy and feel the need to throw them out of bed before they have a chance to Facebook friend request me!" The gays who are lucky enough to be in LTRs stick out among us like golden gods. We wonder how they did it and *pray* for an invite to their next dinner party.

It gets worse because of straight guys who aren't actually straight. When I was beginning my gay adventure, I was naïve enough to dabble in straight-boy dick because I assumed it'd be a fun and sexy challenge. Big mistake. It's never fun to be with someone who still isn't sure what gets them off. God forbid you ever develop feelings for them. You'll lose so much valuable time trying to get them to love you back. The last time I hooked up with a straight boy, he cried and made me promise not to tell anyone. It was then that I knew it was time to only be with boys who liked themselves enough to not sob after a BJ.

It gets worse if you're not living in LA, San Francisco, or New York. I've been fortunate enough to be able to live in my own progressive geographical bubble since I graduated from high school, but many other gay dudes aren't. Not every gay man can just make out in front of a falafel stand at one in the morning. The only reason I'm able to is because I spend an exorbitant amount of money on rent. Whenever I'm making out with a dude in public and get a little nervous, I just think to myself, "Fuck it, Ryan. You pay good money to make out with strangers wherever you want."

It gets worse when you talk to a straight dude and see their wheels start to turn. Finally, they look at you and say, "You know, you're pretty cool for a gay guy." You're supposed to take this as a compliment when, in reality, he just insulted you.

It gets worse when you walk into a gay bar and get stared down by guys who are a pinch cuter than you. Like, they're a little bit skinnier, a little bit more gorgeous, and now you want to just crawl into a ball of sweatpants and Internet porn instead of trying to convince someone you're worthy of a hookup.

It gets worse if you don't go to the gym. Gay men are expected to be born with two things: a giant penis and a six-pack. If we don't have one or both of those things, you can probably find us drunk at some piano bar, huddled around one another in gay average-body-and-penis solidarity.

There's no getting around it: Being gay is weird. Being gay is hard. It's not all fabulous and chic and blow jobs. Sometimes I feel like I have two jobs—there's Ryan, the writer, and Ryan, the homosexual. And guess what? Neither of them come with health insurance. There's immense pressure to adhere to the prevailing standard of gayness. There are "good gays" and "bad gays"—people who are really thriving at their job as a gay man and those who might get laid off soon. Who made these rules? The television—duh! Growing up with TV characters like Jack McFarland from *Will & Grace* and reality shows like *Queer Eye for the Straight Guy* taught us how to be the kind of gay person who's accepted in society, and now we're dealing with the repercussions. We have girls coming up to us wanting to be our friend for novelty and saying things like, "Ugh, I need a gay best friend. Tell me I'm pretty. Tell me I'm fat. Let's make out!"

On top of being treated like this year's hottest accessory by women, we're also inundated with gay teens looking miserable and sobbing all over TV about how "great" it is to come out of the closet, and then we have celebrities telling us that it will all get better one day. And for some people, they're right. The bullied gay kid from Iowa will probably graduate from high school and move to a metropolitan city where he can be himself and form his own big gay family. Eventually he'll get a dog, a boyfriend, a favorite gay bar, and that will be that.

But some of this feels bogus. You can't just Scotch tape a ribbon to a pretty package and pass it off as homosexuality. The reality is that being gay is complicated. You can be here, you can be queer, but you can also have trouble dealing with it. Even the proudest gay men have a certain level of self-loathing about who they are.

Figuring out who you are as a gay man and what group you belong to is a major conundrum. Are you a skinny little thing who can be thrown around in the bedroom? Congrats—you're a twink! Are you big and hairy? You must be a bear! A bear in training is called a cub, which means that because of his age, he's not as big or hairy as a traditional bear. A leather daddy is an older, larger gentleman who . . . likes leather. And a furry is . . . something no one needs to know about.

Jesus. What happened to just being skinny or fat? We have a label for every sort of body type so we can quickly identify exactly what it is that we're into and then run off with it into a subculture. You have twinks fucking cubs fucking bears fucking daddies. It's exhausting to keep up. "I'm a vers/top pref into domination and water sports with uncut straight-acting submissive." Um, what about "I'm a nice person looking for another nice person to grow old with so I don't die alone"? No? Too broad?

You'd think that with all these different types of gay men, I would've encountered a gay guy with a disability at some point, but I haven't. I know they exist, because I'll Google "queer crip" (not a gang, although it'd be amazing if it were) and find all these web forums full of gay men who are paralyzed in wheelchairs or have some other debilitating ailment that are looking for a connection. I feel strange looking at their photos like I'm supposed to have found my tribe, because I don't feel a kinship with them at all. It's that feeling that I'm not disabled enough to identify with other people who have handicaps but also not "normal" enough to pass in the able-bodied world. If I hang out with the gays who have physical handicaps, I'll fancy myself functional. However, if I hang out with the gays who don't have a disability, I'll feel like such a gimp. When I moved to San Francisco, I became uncomfortable being around other gay dudes for reasons beyond my disability. I was worried they would think I was doing a bad job at being gay. Since I wasn't having sex or working out or dancing in da club with my giant gay family, I must be a sad slice of tragic.

Nothing made me feel more like a failure than the fact that I wasn't having sex. I have this idea in my head that everyone is out there living some fabulous gay life except for me. I'm listening to shoegaze in bed while everyone else is getting multiple blow jobs at some amazing elitist gay party. Where's my invite? I don't know if I even want to go. I just want to feel included.

If enough time passes without intimacy, you start to

become fearful of it. It's a vicious cycle. You stop having sex until the point where it becomes a frightening concept and then you stay away. Anal sex is an especially intimate act. As far as I'm concerned, my asshole is reserved for VIPs only. Otherwise, sex feels invasive and cheap. I hear about men who will bend over for anyone and anything—vegetable, animal, mineral—and I'm shocked. Part of me is slut-shaming them out of my own insecurities, and the other part is jealous that they don't attach meaning to every little thing like I do. It must be nice to be able to stop thinking for a second and just do.

That's why being gay is gay for me. I see so many other men falling into bed with each other, forming their gay groups and going to their gay brunches, and I'm here in analysis paralysis land, thinking too much to participate in any of it. I don't want to be promiscuous. I feel things too intensely, so it would just be bad for me, but I need to find a balance where I don't feel like I'm wasting my youth because of fear.

I liked to think that I was special for having a unique set of hardships ("I AM THE ONLY GAY GIMP TO EVER EXIST!"), but the fact is that every gay guy is reconciling how they should be in the eyes of society with how they really are. I'm a gay guy with cerebral palsy. So what? The line forms at the left with the gay guys who feel inadequate.

This was an important thing for me to realize. It's perhaps the best lesson I could have ever taught myself. Getting it would eventually be the one thing that released me from my neuroses and let me be truly happy.

I'm not special.

Finding Love (and Losing It) in a Sea of "Likes"

IF BEING GAY GAVE me my first inkling that I wasn't special, then dating made me feel like a basic bitch without a prayer. Case in point: Recently a boy I had feelings for wrote me a handwritten letter. It was four pages long, written on crisp white paper that crinkled like dead leaves. I read every line hoping it'd contain some wild declaration of love, but instead I got the opposite. At the end of the third page, he wrote, "I'm sorry that I can't love you."

Deep down I already knew this. We had spent the last few months hanging out together, and every time I would leave him, I'd have a feeling this was going to end in tears. I'm not a clairvoyant. I just know these kinds of things. We all do. People owe us nothing: they can blow through our lives, make us feel hopeful and loved, and then disappear with no explanation or apology. This is just the way it is now. There are so many new and exciting ways to get rejected: getting swiped to the left on Tinder, unfriended on Facebook, and ignored on OkCupid. Are we unlovable? No, but we place all our self-worth in getting a text back from our crush, and if it doesn't happen, we automatically assume we're going to die alone.

To counteract this constant fear of rejection, I do what everybody else does: I look for validation by outsourcing my self-esteem to the Internet and various apps. I take selfies until I land on a picture where I look semi-attractive. Then I apply a filter, which will graciously take my looks from a five or six to an eight. By posting the selfie, I ask the world, "Am I attractive? Could you understand if someone made the decision to love me?" I watch with bated breath as the "likes" pile up like little ants giving me their tacit approval. But a like isn't enough for me anymore. I need someone to type, "Looking good!" or "Wow, Mr. Handsome!" to feel fully satisfied.

After posting the selfie, I'll think of something amusing to tweet. Instagram selfies are meant to make you feel pretty, whereas Twitter is designed to validate your intelligence. That's why you follow hot models on Instagram and dowdy comedians on Twitter. It's a necessary separation of brain and brawn. After spending minutes crafting something brilliant, I'll send it out into the universe like a proud parent watching their child graduate. Seeing it get retweeted hits me with a burst of joy that leaves as quickly as it came.

As I'm going to bed, I'll make the final stop in my

Validation Tour by going on gay sex apps like Grindr, SCRUFF, and GROWLr—which is like Grindr but for hairy chubby people. On Grindr and SCRUFF, I'm completely invisible, drowned out by a sea of six-packs and chiseled physiques, but on GROWLr I'm practically Ryan fucking Gosling. My body type is ideal for bears: soft in the middle and hairy but still lean in the way that most younger guys are. The second I log on I'm inundated with messages by men looking to meet up or swap photos. If I find one of the men to be attractive, I will unlock my private photos, which includes a picture of me in briefs. The guy will usually respond with a "SEXY" or a "WOOF" before unlocking his own private photos. I'll take a look at them and if I like what I see, I'll tell him so as I begin to masturbate. The guy will then push for a meet up, but I'll never do it. This is just free porn for me. I look at the naked photos of a man who lives only 1,263 feet away, and instead of meeting him in person, I jack off alone in bed. I have no interest in having an IRL interaction, because I know the second it's over, I'll hate myself.

One time I did meet up with a man off GROWLr. I had just downloaded the app and was feeling extra adventurous. I'd always hooked up with men who had string cheese bodies, so the prospect of being with someone who was big and thick excited me. After only being on the app for a moment, this man messaged me and said, "Hey, cutie . . ."

I looked at his profile picture. His face wasn't a dream but his body, which was practically naked, was flawless. I wrote back: "What's up?"

"Nothing. Just ran errands, walking back to my apartment."

"Cool. Where you at?"

"Curson and Sunset."

Clouded by horniness, I gave him my address and told him to come over. Within minutes, he was at my door. It was so strange. The whole process felt like ordering a pizza.

The man looked at me and smiled. "I don't usually move this quickly." He had a softer voice than I had imagined. You think all big, burly men are going to have this throaty growl—hence the name, GROWLr—but sometimes they sound like delicate flowers. Trying to be aggressive and slutty, I grabbed his face and started making out with him. His tongue thrashed in my mouth and reminded me of a disgusting salamander, but I tried to ignore it. In that moment, I was committed to playing the part of someone who could handle empty sexual encounters.

It was in the middle of a heat wave in Los Angeles, so we were both sopping wet after only a few minutes of hooking up. To cool down, we kept taking breaks and having forced conversation. We'd go at it, get too hot, and have to ask how each other's day was. My gut impression was that this stranger was nice but a little depressed. He was in his late thirties and kept talking about how all of his friends were married and had kids. "I spend a lot of time alone," he told me. "I use the sites to meet friends, but everyone ends up flaking on me after the first hookup."

My desire to have a meaningless sexual encounter was not coming to fruition. The more we talked, the more human he became. Eventually we just stopped hooking up altogether. When he left, he kissed me good-bye and asked to hang out again. I lied and told him yes. A few days later, he messaged me on GROWLr, except this time I didn't respond. Here I was, another person who had disappointed him. Here he was, another person for me to forget.

In high school and college, I didn't have to go on the Internet to get my sexual fix, because I dated real, live boys who spent the night in my apartment and got coffee with me in the morning and met my friends and knew my history. Boys who, in my eyes, actively tried to love me but couldn't because I was fighting them every step of the way.

One such boy was named Corey. We met my senior year of college at a close friend's dinner party. (A dinner party in college meant drinking cheap wine instead of vodka and someone attempting to make a kale salad while wearing a sophisticated polka-dot dress.) Corey came late to the party, drenched in sweat from biking over the Williamsburg Bridge. I had stalked his Facebook profile before and thought he was cute.

That night we all got very, very drunk, and Corey and I ended up kissing in the hallway of my apartment. I convinced myself that I liked him. I was doing that thing people sometimes do when they trick themselves into having feelings for someone just so they can feel more a part of things. For our first date, we got stoned and went to a midnight showing of *The Shining*. He came home with me afterward, and we made out until our faces melted off.

"I am obsessed with Corey," I told my friend Alex over lunch the next day in the East Village.

Alex scrunched up her nose as if she'd just smelled something rotten. "Babe, are you sure? He's an urban studies major and interested in, like, sustainable organic farming. I don't think you two have a lot in common."

"That stuff doesn't matter," I protested, stabbing lettuce with my fork. "He's cute, smart, and funny. I have a good feeling about it!"

Corey and I spent the whole week after our first date texting each other flirty nonsense. Meanwhile, I started to project all my fantasies onto him. In my head, Corey was a dream man. He had all the desirable qualities one looks for in a mate. I mean, I thought he did. I didn't actually know because we'd just met, but I had a hunch!

After a few days of texts and light LOLs, Corey invited me to a party on his rooftop in Bushwick. Ecstatic, I texted back a nonchalant "Sure, sounds cool" and immediately began planning the night out in my head. I'd arrive with a nice bottle of wine ($12), in a pair of shorts that provided easy access for hand jobs, and instead of spending all my time talking to Corey, I'd focus on his friends and get them to fall in love with me first. Then, when the party would start to peter out, I'd swoop in and make my move.

Unfortunately, things didn't go exactly the way I imagined them. By the time I showed up to Corey's rooftop, he was tripping on mushrooms (rude!) and mistook me for a snow globe. I wanted to be like, "Um, Corey? Remember me? Your future boyfriend?" but it was clear he was dunzo. Frustrated and medium-drunk, I finally grabbed Corey by the arm and made him take me downstairs to his bedroom.

"So, listen, I'm gonna go, but thanks so much for inviting me," I said enthusiastically, rubbing his arm.

"Oh, okay." Corey stared at me with a sleepy grin slapped across his face.

I sighed in annoyance and turned to leave, but then Corey

grabbed me and enveloped me in a bear hug. We stood there in his room for almost a minute with his head buried in my chest and our limbs lazily linked together. The balmy fall breeze wafted in and tickled our necks, and I rubbed my palm in circular motions on the curve of Corey's back. His hair was matted with sweat and he smelled like a garbage can, but I didn't care.

"Goddamn," I thought. "I love loving men."

After that night, I knew I had Corey. I wanted him to be my boyfriend, and now he was. It didn't occur to me until a few weeks in that we had less than zero things to talk about. Oops!

Corey and I dated for four, maybe five, months, but the entire time I felt like I was putting myself through a series of tests. "Ryan, let's see if you can have someone sleep over at your apartment three times a week without it freaking you out." "Ryan, let's see if you can go to the opera with this man and meet his friends and his dog." Every time I accomplished a task, I would give myself a pat on the back. Every time I failed to do something (I never once spent the night at his apartment, for example), I would feel like a defective human being.

My relationship with Corey—and any other boy I dated during that time—was never about *him*. It was always about me. I was deeply insecure and narcissistic, which is a lethal combination for anyone attempting to have a real relationship. Being with boys was a way to see if someone could actually love me despite my handicaps. And when I realized that they could and I felt my self-esteem tank getting full, I'd sabotage the relationship and get rid of them. Granted, maybe

I would've cared more about Corey if we had something in common. But finding a guy I was compatible with was always an afterthought. I just needed somebody, anybody, to date me. I lacked all the qualities necessary to actually have a meaningful relationship, which were selflessness, desire, and the ability to compromise. I realized this after I graduated from college, but by then it felt too late. Dating postcollege is like entering the Wild West. Ditching your narcissism and growing up won't guarantee you a relationship with someone. It won't even guarantee you a text message.

There are ten thousand rules instructing Millennials on how to date, many of which contradict each other and make no sense. Here are the ones that everybody follows:

1. **Know how to give good text message.** The definition of a good texter is someone who knows the difference between sending someone an "Okay!" versus an "OK" and who would never dare to send something flirty without consulting a team of experts first. See the following thought process for reference: "If I text this guy I just went on a date with, 'Let me know if you want to hang again sometime,' do I leave things too open-ended? Maybe I should be more assertive and just text 'Let's hang out sometime. What's your schedule like?' That would force him to respond, right?" Every word, grammar, and punctuation choice means something. We spend more time composing the Perfect Text than we do working on our résumés.
2. **The phone call is a major leading cause of terror in twentysomethings.** It's best not to call the person

you're dating unless you're dying, and even then it's a little unclear. I mean, do you *really* think you're dying? And if so, is it really worth jeopardizing something that could be special with a human-to-human phone call? People would rather text an ex, eat glass, and self-identify as a hipster than dial numbers on a phone that will lead you to a person's voice.

3. **Until you have the exclusivity talk, you must assume that the person you're dating is still sleeping with other people.** Even if it's not true, it's always better to minimize expectations to avoid being disappointed. Back in the day, someone was considered a gentleman if they opened the door for you or paid for your dinner. Now it's chivalrous if someone doesn't give you an STD from the person they've been fucking on the side.
4. **DON'T BE DESPERATE.** If your crush knows that you aren't too keen on dying alone and want to find a life partner, they're going to think you're a clingy psycho, so take it slow. First, open the lines of communication by Gchatting them brief, funny thoughts throughout the day. Pretend the Gchats are like mini–hand jobs being used to get them ready for the main event. After that, you progress to creating inside jokes, which gives the illusion that you are super close. Make sure when doing this, however, that your crush is actually *aware* of the inside joke. You can't just text something nonsensical like, "Okay, DUMPSTER BOY. Ha ha!" when there's no context. The final step is exchanging favorite songs/YouTube clips. By the time you do this, you're basically fucking through the screens of your

MacBook Pros. You don't even really need to meet IRL if you don't want to!

5. **Make sure your Internet persona is in top-notch condition.** If you give someone your name and number, the first thing they're going to do is Google the shit out of you. EVERYONE is a Nancy Drew Internet detective, so make sure your Facebook and Twitter are not a colossal embarrassment. Be a minimalist rather than an oversharer. Keep your Facebook photo album limited to your profile pictures and resist captioning them with descriptions such as "At lunch with my friends" or "Skiing the slopes of Mammoth! So lucky!" Potential mates don't need to know everything about you before the first date. Also worth noting: Don't be that person who lists themselves as "in a relationship with so-and-so" on Facebook. It's tacky TMI, and you'll have a lot of fun changing it back to "single" if you two ever break up. Not only will you be living in a bell jar with a broken heart, but you'll have to read comments from people you barely know saying, "OMG, what happened, girlie? CALL ME ASAP!"

These rules are dripping with self-sabotage, aren't they? We've created a dating culture in which we never say what we really feel. God forbid we admit we actually want to be with someone and call them up on the phone instead of waiting six hours to return a text message. We're constantly afraid of being ourselves. Even when I get comfortable with someone, I'm paranoid that my craziness is going to shine through and I'll get dumped. The whole process is so exhausting. And for what? The people we date when we're young are usually awful. They don't deserve our obsession, tears, and neuroses! If you're in your twenties, chances are you have dated one (or all) of these terrible people:

THE THIRTY-FIVE-YEAR-OLD MAN-CHILD WITH A HUGE DICK

The man-child is typically very attractive and wears lots of flannel and age-inappropriate footwear. You would never guess he's thirty-five (and newly divorced from a fellow artist type named Ursula), but the bags under his eyes ultimately give him away. A man-child has to date a decade (or two) younger because any girl in his age group would run away screaming. Certain girls love to date him, though, because they claim to be attracted to men who are creative. The real reasons, however, stem from a deep-seated desire to piss off their well-to-do parents and have as much amazing sex as humanly possible. That's the one good thing about dating a man-child—they're fantastic lays and their dicks are humongous, which makes sense because only someone with a Dirk Diggler shlong can get away with acting so immature and helpless. Remember: a big penis doesn't pay the rent. Usually.

THE PERSON YOU ACCIDENTALLY DATE FOR FOUR MONTHS BECAUSE IT WAS COLD OUT

Have you ever found yourself feeling totally bored and accidentally dating a dud . . . for four months? You're not quite sure how it happened—you were only supposed to hook up a few times—but here you are cuddling and watching the snow fall from your window together. You wonder, "How did this happen? Was I really too lazy to buy a new winter coat this year so I used a human body instead?" The answer is yes, you bum. You can only casually date a person for so long. There comes a point where you have to either make it exclusive or get rid of them entirely. In my experience, the four-month mark is usually when you decide if you want to transition into spring with this person.

THE PSYCHO BITCH

The psycho bitch is sort of like Glenn Close's character in *Fatal Attraction* but infinitely worse because he or she is able to send you text messages. Dating someone who's unstable is not only a headache; it's a total amateur move. People usually get them out of the way in their first or second relationship. It's better to experience the highs and lows early on when you don't know who you are or what you want and you actually have the energy to fight. I can't imagine dating a psycho bitch now. I don't even have the stamina to put on my psoriasis medication, let alone validate someone's feelings every five seconds.

THE STONER

It's practically mandated by God that, at some point in our lives, we spend time sitting in someone's crappy apartment and watching them do bong rips while watching *Family Guy*. How do stoners get laid so often? They're so lazy and weird, and yet somehow, they're always swimming in sex. I don't get it. Do I need to talk more about the bizarre shape of a Cheeto in order to have sex with someone?

THE PERSON YOU DATE IN COLLEGE WHO RUINS YOU FOREVER

Having a relationship in college is like living in a dreamworld. You spend every waking moment together and seriously entertain the idea of moving in together. It feels like this could be the one, but—oops!—it's not. After you graduate, the relationship fails to translate to real life, and you're stuck with someone who feels like a soggy appetizer that's meant to tide you over until the main entrée. Eventually you break up and spend the better part of your twenties getting over it.

THE PERSON YOU'RE ASHAMED TO BE DATING SO YOU DOWNPLAY THE RELATIONSHIP TO YOUR FRIENDS AND HOPE NO ONE FINDS OUT

"He's just a friend! We're not dating! I would never date him. I mean, are you kidding me?" Cut to ten minutes later when your friends leave and you call the Shame Crush and tell him to come over and bring pita chips. Everyone sleeps with someone they're hesitant to bring around their friends. The best thing you can do when you're sleeping with someone you're ashamed of is to be honest and tell your friends, "Listen, guys. I'm sort of with this dude, but it will be over when my depression and/or boredom lifts. Just stand by until I feel normal enough to dump him."

THE NICE GUY

I'm not talking about the type of person who is kind and genuine. I'm talking about a guy who has no discernible quality other than being nice. He's a bland scoop of vanilla ice cream and you are the sun that is melting him down to mush. Nice guys will turn you into a person who's mean, a person who's a bully, a person who points out the flaws, because there needs to be somebody in the relationship who isn't loving blindly. Nice guys don't look at you through a critical lens; they love deeply and stupidly, like you're a puppy and they're just looking for a man's best friend. You could be anyone, really. They don't care. They just want to love something. And they like it when you push them down. They need that. When I date a nice guy, it always ends the same way. I hate them for being so pure, and then I hate myself for being so dirty.

YOUR EX

I know what you did last summer and the summer before that. It was your ex—the person whom you still text when you're drunk at 4:00 a.m., being like, "Beb? R u there? Just missing you. Cum over if u want. No pressure. I'm so wasted . . ." It's important to let them know you're wasted so they know you're not in your right mind. Then you wait for their response, which will either be, "Okay, be right there!" or "WTF? Um, no . . ." If you're "lucky" and get the former response, you're setting yourself up for sex that can continue for a shockingly long time. Sometimes it won't stop until you get into a new relationship, proving that in order to get over certain people, you need to get under someone else.

THE EMOTIONALLY CLOSED-OFF ASSHOLE

If you haven't *been* the asshole in the relationship, chances are you've *dated* the asshole. There are so many terrible things about dating someone who's emotionally distant and puts you down in subtle, creepy ways, but perhaps the worst thing is that you honestly believe you can change them. It can take years/forever (#dark) for you to realize that it's just not in the asshole's DNA to be sweet. Those rare moments of tenderness they show you are just tricks to keep you around longer. You'll never be good enough. They hate your friends, the clothes you wear, and the things you choose to talk about. But most of all, they just hate themselves.

THE PERSON YOU DIDN'T REALIZE YOU WERE ACTUALLY DATING

Since we're all a bunch of commitment-phobes, we often end up in the gray area with the people we date, which is a terrible place to be for everyone! If you're the person who's getting sent mixed signals, you're resigned to being an insecure wreck until you're given some definitive answers. You're clutching your phone like it's a lifeline and going into full-body spasms whenever you get a new text message. If you're in a position of power and keeping things loose and vague, it can still suck because you risk having someone think you're actually together when you're simply dating. Before you know it, you'll be getting an "in a relationship" request from someone you can't even bring yourself to text back in a timely manner.

We date these people who aren't right for us to learn more about ourselves or because we want to have a story to tell our friends at brunch or because we think it's better than being alone. But dating someone who doesn't get you will make you feel more alone than ever. Also, don't think for one second that these relationships are meaningless. Every one-night stand, every insult, every fight, every orgasm has gotten you to where you are right now, which might be sitting alone in your apartment x-ing out of OkCupid and opening another bottle of wine. These are the consequences of not treating yourself with care.

Sometimes when it's been a long time since I've been with someone, I'll think back to being seventeen and taking a shower with my then boyfriend, Charlie. We'd usually take them together after we had sex to wash the smell off our bodies and talk about whatever things seventeen-year-old gay boys like to talk about. Charlie would casually put a dollop of shampoo in his palm and rub it in my hair, taking an extra second to massage my scalp, and I would do the same for him. The mundaneness of these showers would often leave me feeling overwhelmed with emotion because I realized, with a clarity that made my stomach drop, that this was intimacy. Feelings of closeness rarely occurred during sex, like I expected them to, but rather in the afterglow. The postcoital silences that were peppered with the short staccato blasts of breathing, the tenderness you can feel when someone does something as simple as hand you a bar of soap in the shower. These were the moments that taught me how to love someone, and when I remind myself of it, I know that I can relearn intimacy. I can have brave love that's dripping with vulnerability. I can have love that won't dissolve because of a shitty text message, a love without deal breakers. When I was seventeen, I was raw and naïve with zero emotional baggage. Nothing held me back from saying what I felt, because I didn't know the rules to the games people like to play. Then, somewhere between a string of failed flings in college and embarrassing attempts at dating after I graduated, I became so ruled by my own insecurities and thirst for validation that I missed the point of relationships and forgot how to have a partner. Sometimes I look at my friends who are in stable, healthy relationships and I'm overcome with envy. They did it. They figured out how to wake up in the morning with someone without feeling the urge to run away. They realized they were worth loving. Having self-love is like nurturing a plant. If you don't take the time to water it, if you start to skip days and get distracted, it will die.

Believing that you deserve love is not only imperative for finding a relationship; it's also crucial for getting out of one.

As far as I can tell, there are three guarantees in life: death, taxes, and someone deciding they don't love you anymore. I can pinpoint the exact moment Charlie lost all interest in me. We were lying in my bed one day after school trying to have sex before his parents picked him up (oh the joys of being underage and sexually active!), but something was preventing us from fully connecting. His body, which had usually felt like a second home to me, was distant and rigid. I asked him what was wrong. He assured me it was nothing, but the way he said it made it seem like it was *everything*. It was then that I knew we existed on borrowed time. A few weeks later, Charlie dumped me.

The takeaway message from getting dumped is that a person who once wanted to see you naked all the time is now no longer interested in seeing you at all. Just like that. "I want your private parts in my mouth" to "Get those private parts away from me right now before I call the cops!" Part of you wants to say back to them, "Wait! I wasn't done having sex with you yet. Can you give me a bit more time?" But there is no more time left to give.

I always wonder how this can happen. Like, how do you go from loving someone despite their bad breath and rolls of fat and IBS to all of a sudden being like, "Nope. I can no longer tolerate the flaws. I look at you and instead of feeling a warmth, my bones start to chill." How? If I knew the answers to any of these questions, perhaps breakups would be easier for me to handle, but since I don't, it's difficult for me to get over anyone I've ever had feelings for.

I've dated a healthy amount. I've been with assholes, nice guys, and everything in between, but I've never actually been in a serious relationship before. One day, while at happy hour after work, my coworkers and I got on the subject of exes, and one asked me point-blank, "Have you ever been in a serious relationship?" The question left me stunned, like I didn't quite know the answer because, in some ways, it feels like I have. I've had my heart broken and dated people for respectable stretches of time. Still, none of my love-life adventures have ever amounted to much. I blame part of my inexperience on the fact that I wasted so much time being hung up on Charlie after our breakup. I was so desperate to have him in my life that I was like, "Don't worry about dumping me and causing my whole world to go down in flames. Let's just stay best friends, okay?" He agreed, and voilà—that's how you get years of pretending that you want friendship instead of "I love you" and a warm dick in your ass. I wasn't thinking clearly. You never are after a breakup. You have to pretend that everything is fine when secretly you're dying a thousand deaths a minute. It was especially hard in the beginning. I would have delusional thoughts that I couldn't vocalize to anyone, such as, "Oh, there's a hair salon. My ex had hair!" or "How do I steer this conversation in a direction where my ex gets mentioned? I know my friends are tired of hearing about him, but if I don't say his name at least five times a day, I run the risk of becoming very ill. Oh, great—they're talking about the weather. There's my in."

I kept Charlie in my life for so long because I needed to hang on to the proof that somebody once loved me. "See?" I'd fantasize telling people after we broke up, "A guy actually called me his boyfriend once. You can ask him yourself if you don't believe it." I didn't want to move on. That would mean I'd have to look for someone else to date me, and it was doubtful that such a person existed. Charlie was a fluke. Anyone else would see my scars, my limp, my tight legs and hunched-over back and find me grotesque.

When I moved to New York for school, Charlie and I finally began to drift apart. I stopped calling him, and since he never really called me, that was enough to end us. Now I haven't spoken to him in years, but because this is the digital age, he's still hanging around. We're friends on Facebook, and we recently followed each other on Twitter. A few weeks after receiving a notification that he'd followed me, I tried to direct-message him only to find out that he had already unfollowed me. Blind with rage, I texted him, "You unfollowed me on Twitter? Really?" He quickly responded with, "I'm sorry. I just think it's better this way. Please don't take it personally." Even though I understood why Charlie wanted to delete me from his social media—you don't need to know that the guy you lost your virginity to is eating roast chicken for dinner—it still stung. Technology has made it impossible for us to really say good-bye. When my mother was nineteen, she married a man, divorced him two years later, and hasn't heard from him since. Isn't that nuts? The thought of marrying someone today and then being like, "Bye. Lose my number!" seems inconceivable. I don't even have the luxury of forgetting a guy I hooked up with a few times when I was twenty-one because I keep seeing pictures of him drinking stupid mimosas with his stupid friends on Facebook. He won't disappear. He's not allowed to and neither is Charlie. They'll always be only a few keystrokes away. Breaking up with someone now just means the end of physical contact.

They live on everywhere else—on your computers, in your phones, in texts. We lost our right to move on from people when we decided we wanted to know everything about everyone. And it's not just our lovers who haunt us like virtual ghosts. It's also our friends. In your twenties, you expect to accumulate a graveyard's worth of failed romances. But what you don't count on is having to bury so many treasured friendships alongside them.

Best Friends Forever, Best Friends Never

It's 1:58 p.m. on a Saturday. Do you know where your friends are?

—Socrates (JK, hon—that was me!)

I met my best friend Clare when I was a social butterfly spreading its emotionally slutty wings at college. Our mutual friend Bianca had wanted to introduce us for quite some time, but I didn't put much stock into it. If I had a nickel for every time a person wanted me to meet someone they thought I'd like, I'd be making friendship bracelets out of hundred-dollar bills. But one day, during a break between classes, Clare and I ran into each other in the quad. She complimented me on my jacket. I told her thank you and then we decided to be best friends forever. At that age, starting a lifelong friendship can be that simple. Your heart is open and you're desperate for some kind of closeness. The dipshit boys you're hooking up with at house parties only fill the void in your private parts. If you want a deep connection, you have no choice but to turn to your friends. They're the ones who'll make you come every time.

The summer after Clare and I graduated from college, she moved into an apartment near me in Alphabet City, and we spent every day in her courtyard drinking wine and talking until our brains turned into happy goo. We were in the throes of friend love, blissfully killing time together before our real lives started. That's what you do when you're twenty-two. You murder time like it's a disgusting bug. Now you'll do anything to keep it alive.

Shortly after our first postgrad summer came to a close, Clare canceled our OMG-I'm-obsessed-with-you friendship tour by getting a boyfriend who wasn't just another liberal arts loser. Dylan was a guy who would text her back on time, make her feel safe, and not judge her if she actually needed him. It changed everything. Gone were the languid days of Clare and me sitting in her courtyard. In their place were obligatory catch-up lunches and emotionally charged text messages.

"Wanna hang out Saturday?" I asked Clare on the phone one day.

"I think so. But I have yoga and then Dylan and I are going to meet his parents for dinner. Could you hang from one to three?"

Oh, fuck no. "Really? When did we become the kind of friends who scheduled each other in two-hour blocks of time?"

Clare argued back, explaining that I made her feel guilty

when she couldn't live up to my high expectations of being a friend. She was right. I was feeding into some sad fag hag–gay man cliché of codependency. The straight girl finds love. The gay boy remains alone and spiteful. But it's hard to watch your friends grow up before you do. Clare and I initially bonded over being emotional lushes, but when she got into a relationship, she figured her life out while I stayed the same mess I'd always been. It was mortifying to be the only one who wanted things to go back to the way they were.

"You know I wasn't happy then, Ryan," Clare told me recently. "I was drinking too much and dating assholes. You're romanticizing a very dark time."

Maybe I was. But I wasn't expecting my friendships to change this fast. Growing up, I thought my twenties were going to be like the television show *Friends*. After college, my best buddies and I would get a beautiful apartment in Manhattan, despite the fact that none of us had decent jobs, and we'd spend our days having friendship orgies. When we couldn't scrounge up enough money for rent, we'd pay for it using the sheer power of our bonds. "You guys," the landlord would address us wearily, "you need to stop sending me checks that just have 'LOVE!' scribbled across them. I can't cash these!" On the rare occasion that my roommates and I would leave our cozy apartment, it'd be to lie on coffee shop couches and commiserate about the sad state of our love lives for nineteen hours. Everything in the world would disappoint us—except for each other!

Well, maybe it wouldn't be that much of a culty lovefest, but I at least thought I'd have someone to dance with in my room after a long day at work. Instead, I found myself with a lot of paper-thin friendships. Whenever I'd have a connection with someone and attempt to make plans, we'd get lost in a black hole of texting. They'd be like, "Hey, I really enjoy your company but I'm too weird to set up an actual friend date so I will just continue to text with you 24/7 and make vague references to hanging out IRL even though we both know that will never come to fruition!"

Then there are the people I used to be close with but then something happened—no one's sure what—and now we've become people who just check in with each other occasionally. Lame attempts to hang out are made, but it rarely ever happens. A friend will text me, "It's offensive how long we've gone without seeing each other. This is not okay!" and I'll be like, "OMG, I know. Hang time ASAP, plz!" But we both know it means nothing.

Your best friend, the one who manages to stick with you during the apocalypse that is your twenties, is the person who saves you from all of this misery. The bond you have is so authentic and loving that it almost feels criminal to have it in the modern age. When you're together, you spend hours having brain orgasms. You can bring this friend anywhere—to a dive bar or an intimidating club—and they always make you feel safe. You never have to worry about them. There's none of the usual friendship maintenance. You could go months without seeing each other and pick up right where you left off.

Unfortunately, a best friend is not guaranteed. You think it is. You grow up waiting for the moment someone comes along and becomes the Daria to your Jane, but it doesn't always happen. I've met people—normal, delightful people—who bristle when you ask about their friendships. They'll say, "I'm friends with a lot of people, but I don't know if I have, like, a best friend." You know what they mean when they say that. A "best friend" is someone who, when asked which person sees the world the same way you do, will say your name without hesitation. There's no anxiety about the feelings not being entirely mutual. You can write their name confidently in blood.

I've been lucky enough to have a few special friendships, but the one that was most important to me is also the one I lost. I met Sarah in the Foothill Tech cafeteria when we were frightened freshman babies. We both looked at each other and were like, "Hi, nice to meet you. Want to get through this hell together?" She was a six-foot-tall water polo player with a metal rod in her back. I was a gay gimp with bad skin and rainbow hair. Separately, Sarah and I didn't stand a chance at loving high school, but when we combined forces, everything was golden. We did everything together. We volunteered at the LGBT youth center and taught young gays that safe sex meant more than just doing it somewhere your parents couldn't find you. We wrote plays about the absurd social politics of high school and performed them for our drama class. We even tried to be evolved like the French and shared a boyfriend for a few months. (No threesomes, obviously—just lots of slutty swapping with a bisexual hippie who had a big dick.) After high school ended, Sarah and I went away to different colleges, but we lived together every summer, interning and writing scripts. Our plan was to write a few sample specs before moving out to LA to pursue careers as television writers.

Of course, life never works out the way you want it to. During our sophomore year of college, Sarah was diagnosed with ovarian cancer and spent the fall and most of the spring semester undergoing chemo. She recovered a few months later, right around the same time I was hit by a car in San Francisco. We intended to go to New York for the summer to take a screenwriting class, but we were both too depressed to do anything, so we decided to sublet an apartment in Los Angeles and spend the next few months processing our respective mindfucks-of-a-year. I was convinced it was going to play out like a sequel to *Girl, Interrupted*. (*Girl, Still Interrupted*? Somebody get my agent on the phone!) There'd be no sun-drenched barbecues, swim days, or steamy summer romances. Sarah and I would just lie in bed, sobbing into a bottle of Xanax.

That's what *should've* happened, anyway. I spent almost every day working on my hand in physical therapy and couldn't move my fingers or make a fist. Meanwhile, Sarah was still experiencing terrible side effects from chemo. The two of us were a bona fide goof troop. But instead of resigning ourselves to a sad existence, we made an unspoken agreement to spend our summer having LOLs for breakfast, lunch, and dinner. We went out to parties, even though I was still in an arm cast and could barely hold my drink. We explored different parts of LA. We tried to get laid. It was like every other magical summer, except with a dash of emotional trauma.

If our friendship could survive cancer and my accident and still be stronger than ever, you'd think we'd have it made. But sometime between that summer in LA and college graduation, something changed between us. Our lives, once nearly identical, started to take different shapes. Sarah got into a serious relationship. I moved to New York for school and found a whole new group of friends. Since the beginning of our friendship, our identities had been inextricably linked, but as we got older, we realized we didn't need each other as much. I depended on Sarah to tell me who I was, but when I started getting more comfortable in my own skin, I began to define myself on my own.

Sarah and I lived together one last time right before we graduated. We moved into another apartment in LA so we could write a spec script. The first one we wrote had gone swimmingly, but this experience was gut-wrenchingly bad. Our chemistry was off from day one, and we could never find proper footing with each other. Every day we would try to sit and write, but there was no creative synergy between us. It was like watching something I love get destroyed in slow motion. I wanted to scream, "Freeze! Stop turning my best friend into a complete stranger!" but there was nothing either of us could do. Time was going to murder us.

Right before we moved out, I dropped a bomb on Sarah. "I'm not sure if I'm married to the idea of writing for TV," I told her while packing up my suitcase. "I think I want to stay in New York and maybe explore the advertising world."

Sarah looked up and shot me an "Are you fucking kidding me?" look. She had ditched her boyfriend for the summer so she could be here and write this script, and now I was casually shitting all over our future.

"Really? Advertising? Uh, that's interesting. I've literally never heard you say anything about that before, but cool!"

I didn't actually have a desire to work in advertising, but I thought telling Sarah this would force us to have an honest conversation about why our friendship had deteriorated so much. Unfortunately, it didn't facilitate any discussion. When we went back to school, our phone conversations became more infrequent and stilted. Eventually I met up with her in San Francisco, where she had been living after college (she, too, had given up on the dream of being writing partners in Los Angeles), and told her that we had grown apart. She cried, I cried after she left, and that was that. The most heartbreaking aspect of Sarah and me ending our friendship was that there was no massive betrayal or devastating event that would justify something so special dying. We stopped being friends simply because we became two different people. I was shocked that such a thing could even happen. Sarah and I being friends seemed like the only guarantee in my life, but now I realize how naïve I was for thinking anything was a sure bet. For over two decades, my friends and I were on the same track, achieving important milestones together. Then we graduated from college and started living completely different lives overnight. Of course shit was going to get weird.

After graduation, your friends typically take one of two paths: they either fall into a serious relationship or throw themselves into a career. If you're one of those psychos who can somehow master a job and a relationship right after college, then congratulations and I hate you. For everyone else, what we have here is a division. In one camp, we have people who are devoting all their time to their first serious relationship. This kind of love is more intense than what they experienced in high school and college. They're not just counting down the days with someone until school's out for the summer. They're choosing a person to build a life with.

In the other camp, friends are putting a ring on their job and asking to marry it. Unless someone's a prostitute or a porn star, I'm pretty sure their job can't give them blow jobs, but what it lacks in sexiness it makes up for in mental stimulation. They're discovering the things they're good at and understanding their value as a worker. If only they had half the energy to dedicate to their personal life as they did with their professional, they'd have it made!

Both paths give a person a sense of purpose and security, which is essential for someone who's just left college and has no idea what the hell they're doing. They have to channel all their energy into *something*, and it's really only a matter of what scares them less: a relationship or a job. Funnily enough, both parties are convinced the other person has it better. The friend who's in a solid relationship would kill to have an amazing job, whereas the young professional would like nothing more than to have someone to go home to.

There are also people who have neither the job nor the relationship to fall back on. Being in a postgrad slump is an excuse you can only use for so long before people start to worry about you. "Did you hear about Jessica?" a concerned friend whispers at lunch. "She just got fired from her menial office job and she hasn't left her apartment in a week. She's not even dating anyone! It's sad because, like, we graduated two years ago. It's time to get your shit together, you know?" Yes, I know. You know. And your friend Jessica definitely knows. You need to shut up and exhibit some compassion.

Transitioning to adulthood is hard enough. Having your friends judge your progress doesn't make it any easier.

For a year after college, I was that pitiful friend with no job or dating prospects. When I finally landed a full-time job, I called up all my buddies to inform them that I was a useful person again. "You don't have to worry about me," I'd scream into the receiver. "I'm still in the running to be America's Next Top Adult!" It took me 2.5 seconds to turn into the kind of annoying person who only wanted to talk about their job. I couldn't help myself. My work became my life, and I loved it. But you know the one thing that sucks about being a single career girl? Saturdays and Sundays. What once was a cherished time for respite and fun with my friends was now a dreaded reminder that I wasn't in a relationship. When did weekends unofficially become regarded as couple time? It feels like it happened overnight. One weekend I was lying in bed hungover with my best friends, living, laughing, and loving, and the next I was receiving text messages like, "Sorry, can't hang! At the flea market with the BF. Hang Tuesday night?" Ah, Tuesday night: the dreaded single-friend time slot. In the hierarchy of time, Saturday afternoons reign supreme and Tuesdays at 7:00 p.m. are a mere pity offering. When can I get back to the coveted weekend time slot? Who do you have to fuck around here to see your friends on a weekend afternoon?

It's not just relationships and jobs that prevent us from seeing our friends. It's also because we're complete flakes. People are always one text away from bailing on you with some bullshit excuse like, "Oh no! I just got super tired. Do you mind if we reschedule? I'll call you if I get a second wind!" Or worse—they'll lie and say they're sick, because they found something better to do. "Don't Instagram this!" they'll hiss to the friend they blew you off for. "I told Julie I got food poisoning, so she can't know that I'm here!" Blowing people off is turning into an epidemic, and it's ruining our personal relationships. All we do is complain about how we miss our friends and feel so isolated, but when it comes time to see someone face-to-face, we freeze up. What the hell is going on here? What's really preventing us from committing to a plan?

I have thousands of Facebook friends and Twitter followers, so one could safely assume that I'd be drowning in playdates, but the opposite is true. It's easy to tweet at a person, and it's easy to "like" their statuses on Facebook, but it's getting harder and harder to actually show up for someone and actively put effort into building a friendship. I find it hilarious that I'm "friends" with so many people on the Internet when I actually only hang out with five people. That's how it works, though. The more fruitful your virtual life is, the more your real life gets neglected. Sometimes I think about the future of my social life and worry that things are going to get even darker. I see myself at my best friend's wedding getting sad drunk at the singles table while people stare and thank God that the lives they have are fuller than mine. After everybody I love gets married, our friendships will be reduced to phone calls and lunches and "I miss you" and "Remember when?" Then babies will enter the picture and everything will be ruined. The only people who will have time to hang out with me are the elderly at a seafood buffet.

When Clare and other close friends of mine fell down the

rabbit hole of a long-term relationship, there was a part of me that felt like I was getting left behind. While I was busy working and sabotaging my love life, they were moving in with their significant others and progressing emotionally in ways that I couldn't even fathom. I wanted to be a part of their life change and they wanted to be a part of mine, but it didn't feel possible. They were in love. They understood things about the world that I didn't, and it had created an undeniable inequity between us.

Clare and I could have stopped being friends like Sarah and I did. The only reason we survived is because we decided to put the work in. After two years of festering resentments, we finally had it out with each other in front of a juice bar in the West Village. We screamed unthinkable things at each other; we took a rusty knife and dug deep into the wounds. Clare sobbed. I sobbed. People drank their juice and were like, "WTF?" By the time it was over, we were like, "Even though I hate you right now, the thought of not being friends makes me hate everything else more." So we agreed to start from scratch and let go of any past anger. We had to. There are so many people in this world who make you feel like an alien. When you find someone who "gets it," you don't take it for granted. Great people don't grow on trees.

I've accepted that my friendships will change as we mature, and it's unhealthy to fight it. Being someone's friend once said more about yourself than you could ever say on your own, but then you grew up and stopped feeling like half a person. This doesn't make friendships less valuable now. If anything, they take on more meaning. Now that you've gotten your sea legs and started to become the person you're going to be, you're not looking for validation or to fill a void. You want to be around people because you like them. Shocking, isn't it? Just chalk it up to another life lesson you only learn through extensive trial and error. It's embarrassing that it's taken me this long to figure out how to navigate something as seemingly easy as friendships, but I can't say that I'm surprised. I feel like there are people who get things on the first try and then there are people like me with a slow learning curve who have to fight long and hard for every inch of growth. I've made a lot of progress in my life, but the one lesson that took me the longest to figure out is the one that almost derailed everything.

I couldn't stop the bad things from feeling so damn good.

How Not to Drink or Do Drugs

BEFORE I LEFT FOR college and embarked on what would be a decade of mistakes, my father sat me down and gave me some typical advice like, "Don't eat soft-serve in the dining hall every day unless you want to gain the freshman fifteen," and "Be sure to invest in a nice pillow to soften the blow of sleeping on a shitty dorm mattress." He also told me that if I drank any alcohol, I'd run the risk of becoming more retarded.

Dad: Ryan, I know college is a time for experimentation and getting drunk, but I really think it's in your best interest to not partake in that stuff.

Me: Come on, Dad. Everyone is going to be drinking.

Dad: Need I remind you that you're not like everybody else?

Me: What do you mean?

Dad: You have brain damage.

Me: I know. So what?

Dad: So what? You don't have the luxury of losing any more brain cells!

Me: Dad, drinking is not going to give me more brain damage.

Dad: It might.

Me: Well, then I don't care. I'm still going to do it!

Dad: That stubbornness is your brain damage talking.

My father's never had a sip of alcohol in his life. He considers it to be low-class behavior and will turn into an instant Judge Judy if someone drinks in front of him. A few years after that conversation, while I was home from college, my father began interrogating me about my partying. I'd just turned twenty-one and moved to New York City, so I obviously wasn't riding the sober train. The first friend I made at Eugene Lang was this crazy lush, Sadie, who only wore Chanel and lived in a luxury apartment building downtown. Every night I spent with her had the potential to be the Best Night Ever, and it usually was. Sadie just attracted insanity. It scared me a little bit, her manic energy and thirst for a never-ending supply of booze and drugs, but it was also thrilling for someone like me who just moved to the city and wanted to feast on YOLOs. A typical night for us meant drinking a bottle of wine before we left her place to go out and then downing as many margaritas as we could stomach at some epic party. By night's end, I was usually passed out on her floor while the rest of my friends stayed up to call their coke dealers and danced around my lifeless corpse. I couldn't tell my dad about any of these shenanigans, though. He'd have an aneurysm, and I'd be strapped to a gurney and sent off to rehab at Broken Promises. So I lied and told him that I only drank once a week.

Dad: ONCE A WEEK? Oh. My. God. Ryan, that's veering into alcoholic territory.

Me: What? No, it's not!

Dad: It's abnormal. No one is drinking that much.

Me: Yes, they are. My drinking is fine, Dad!

I was telling the truth. I've been imbibing for ten years, and even though I've had brief periods of heavy drinking, there's never been a problem. My mother is an alcoholic who's been sober for years. I've accompanied countless friends to A.A. meetings for moral support. I know what alcoholism looks like, and it's not me, hon. My father, however, was convinced I was raging too much. After our little chat, he surprised me a week later with some "proof" that I was spiraling out of control.

Dad: Ryan, I've been thinking a lot about what you *claim* to be a normal amount of alcohol for kids your age to consume. As you know, The Dad loves to research . . .

Me: Oh God. What did you do?

Dad: Nothing major. I just interviewed a group of kids your age about their alcohol consumption.

Me: You're lying. That would require a level of crazy I'm almost positive you don't have.

Dad: I did, and all of the kids I talked to thought getting drunk once a week was excessive.

Me: DID YOU INTERVIEW MORMONS?

Dad: No. These kids were normal. Just like you.

Just like me? As if. My father's "data" was bogus and clearly pooled from sexually active LARPers. Still, his meddling into my relationship with alcohol caused me to reflect on my sordid drunk history.

It all started when I was a senior in high school and took a sip of cheap champagne. It reminded me of the Martinelli's I used to have on New Year's Eve with my parents, and I loved it! I guzzled down the entire bottle and got completely white-girl wasted. When you start your love affair with alcohol, your mind always goes to excess. Why settle for drunk when you can black out, puke on someone, and have a great story to tell the next morning at breakfast? The goal is to get out of control and become the talk of the party. "Oh really? You had sex in your best friend's mom's bed and then vomited all over it? Well, once I was so blacked out I peed in a litter box!" That really did happen to one of my friends. She peed in a litter box. I was there. I saw it. It happened. I saw some other weird things, too. Once I watched a girl sob uncontrollably while making out with her boyfriend in the middle of a house party. Everyone pretended not to notice and danced around them, which is pretty darn polite for a group of seventeen-year-olds. Another time I witnessed a cake fight break out at a birthday party, which completely destroyed the tiles of whoever's house it was. Then, taking a page from the movie *Stand By Me*, everyone started puking rainbow-colored pieces of cake. It actually looked kind of pretty.

This all happened during the first phase of drinking, when alcohol still looked like a goddamn beauty queen and hadn't shown us its ugly face yet. We'd get blissfully fucked-up, do something insane, and face zero consequences. In fact, you'd have an army of friends around you supporting your decisions and making sure you're okay.

"Do you need to puke?" one concerned friend would ask. "I'll pull your hair back when you vomit."

"No, I will!" another friend would interject. "She's my best friend! Let me do it!"

The last time I vomited from drinking I was lying by myself on the cold bathroom floor with no one to bring me saltines or water, and only then did I finally have to admit to myself that times had changed. Like, remember when we didn't even get hangovers? Maybe you'd wake up after a bender and be all, "God, I want to eat a burrito!" but you'd never have the kind of days where you're completely debilitated and can't move or eat until 7:00 p.m. Those come later when you stop believing all the amazing things alcohol had promised you—when parties feel like *Groundhog Day* and sex isn't as exciting and puking is an unfortunate nightmare instead of a badge of honor. When you're a teenager, you want to make things happen, because everything in your life feels so boring. You're desperate for something, anything, to come along and make you feel like you're in some fabulous teen movie. Fast-forward to ten years later when your life has become so bizarre and overwhelming on its own that you wouldn't dare add to the weirdness.

Things were better when we drank for the right reasons. When we wanted to feel close to each other and have new experiences and make new friends. Granted, the experiences weren't always great, and the people you befriended could be total nightmares, but it didn't matter. You could handle the disappointment. I remember barreling through so many parties determined to make the night my bitch. The lure of possibility would keep me going from new person to new person, hoping to make a connection. Finally, I'd meet someone, exchange some banter, and think, "Wow! You're so cool. I want to know more!" Four shots later, I'd blow my load and declare us new BFFs.

"I fucking love you!" I screamed at this girl Samantha, whom I had met thirty minutes earlier at the chips-and-dip section of a house party in college. The two of us instantly bonded over our love of LiveJournal and boys who didn't text us back. High off our newfound closeness, we then proceeded to take 42,069 whiskey shots.

"No, you don't understand. I'm obsessed with you," Samantha slurred back at me. "Give me your number, bitch. We're going to get brunch in six hours!"

"I fucking love brunch," I yelled.

"Fuck yeah, you do! Brunch besties!" Samantha squealed before dragging me into the living room so we could dance to "Fuck the Pain Away" by Peaches.

The next morning, I signed on to Facebook and saw that Samantha had already tagged me in a bunch of unflattering pictures. "UM, I THINK I FOUND MY SOUL

MATE?!!" read one caption. It was a blurry photo of us hugging on the bathroom floor. I clicked on Samantha's profile, expecting an Internet presence similar to mine, but instead I got a shrine to basicness. There were Bible quotes sprinkled everywhere, FarmVille requests, and unclear ex-boyfriends. I untagged the photos immediately and never spoke to Samantha again. It was obvious I'd been wearing white wine–spritzer goggles and had the friendship equivalent of a one-night stand.

When I wasn't drinking to make friends, I was doing it to get laid. In my junior year of college, I hate–hooked up with a boy for four months, but not one of those times was sober. I don't remember a single thing about the sex. His dick could've been two inches or a foot long. I have no idea and, more important, no interest in ever knowing. I didn't like this boy, and I don't think he liked me. And even if I did have feelings for him, I'd probably still need to be drunk to initiate a hookup. I was new at this, and any kind of intimacy felt too real. Being numb was the best way to feel something honestly.

After college, things changed, and it was no longer chic to be a random shit show. You couldn't drink two-dollar wine and pee in the street or scream at your boyfriend anymore. Everyone is too paranoid they don't have their shit together that life has become a pissing contest over who's grown up the most. "Oh God, the things I used to do in college . . ." your friend will tell you, sipping some white wine at happy hour. "Wow. Just wow!" Hold the phone, sister. College wasn't that long ago! Why are we trying to pretend that we're reformed soccer moms? Everyone is still a hot mess. Don't tell me about how great your job is going. Tell me about how you cried last week in a Duane Reade because you were taken off health insurance. That's more relatable.

A few years ago, I met up with a friend whom I used to party with back in college. When we saw each other, he immediately tried to do damage control. "Man, those were some crazy times. I don't rage like that anymore," he insisted. Meanwhile, I was thinking, "Bullshit, bullshit, bullshit. You're about four drinks away from calling your coke dealer." And I was right! A few drinks in, coke got mentioned, and in the blink of a twitching eye, he called his guy to score some blow. "Oh God," he sighed, hanging up his phone. "I can't believe I'm doing this!" Um, I can. You're a twenty-four-year-old buying coke in a Lower East Side bar. The world is not going to fall off its axis.

When his coke dealer came, I got into a time machine back to 2007 and found myself doing bumps in the bathroom at some disgusting bar I hadn't set foot in in years. Then, to add icing to the very mature cake, we ended up getting caught by a bouncer and escorted out of the bar. My friend looked at me with a sheepish grin on his face, apologized for the night going south, and quickly said good-bye. I never saw him again. That night I learned that the more someone tells you they've changed, the more likely they are to still be getting kicked out of bars for doing coke. You can only really grow when you start being honest with yourself about who you are in the first place.

Don't treat life like it's a race. Also, don't ever do coke. Maybe it was the shit back in the '70s and '80s, but now it just makes you shit. You might already know that, though. Millennials have pushed drugs like coke back in the closet, only allowing them to reappear occasionally in a discussion about recovery, but everybody still does them. People aren't supposed to know that your road to adulthood has been paved with eight balls instead of long-term relationships and cute brunches with your friends. Go on the Facebook page of a heavy drug user and you'll see an online identity that's been carefully curated. There are pictures of her smiling with her family on vacation or hiking some canyon in Los Angeles. Then you meet her in real life and discover that she's a wild partier who's snorting pills in her living room and getting wasted every day. My generation is the first to be in charge of their image. We call the shots and tell you how to feel about our lives. It doesn't matter if what we're projecting is phony. If someone believes it, that makes it true.

When I go on Instagram and see people at SoulCycle or snuggling in bed with their dog and significant other, I feel like an insta-loser. I know they're doing what everybody else does, which is cherry-picking the brightest moments while hiding the dark parts, but it still makes me feel bad about myself. I want to institute an Internet honesty day where people tweet and post pictures of what they're really doing. "Just had a delicious brunch (you saw the amazing photos earlier, right?), but now my hangover and IBS have set in, so I'm lying in bed feeling vaguely depressed. Here's a photo of the weed I'm about to smoke . . ." I think it'd be a cathartic exercise. Everyone could see the giant disparity between the lives we feel like we're supposed to be living and our day-to-day reality. Then maybe by realizing that we're all secretly struggling, we wouldn't feel like such failures.

I used to do a fair amount of drugs. It was during a time when I equated coolness with self-destruction. I thought that if something didn't hurt me, it wasn't worth doing. It took me years to realize that not only was this a terrifying way to live but I also should stay the fuck away from mind-altering substances because the two of us don't get along. I was the person who smoked pot and then became paranoid that UFOs were going to come down to steal my soul. I was the guy who took Adderall to study but got distracted looking at his desk lamp for six hours. Nothing demonstrated my ineptitude at taking drugs more clearly than the time I took Molly. I had tried this "pure" form of Ecstasy once before, but it didn't work. I just felt kind of warm and dumb, which is how I feel most of the time anyway. Never one to get discouraged, I bought some more from another dealer and decided to take double the dose at a friend's birthday party. This is a stupid, stupid thing to do—each batch of drugs has a different level of potency—but I wasn't thinking. Like my deceased queen Aaliyah once sang, "If at first you don't succeed, dust yourself off and try a lot more Molly again." So, the night of the birthday party I dissolved a ton of Molly in some water and drank it up in the bathroom of a bar. Then I waited to feel different. And waited. Twenty minutes passed and I still felt sober.

"What the hell is going on?" I asked my friends who had also taken Molly. "Why isn't this working?"

"I have no clue," my friend Jenny said, her eyes rolling to the back of her head. "I feel AMAZING."

I looked over at my other friend Angela, who was googly-eyed and talking animatedly to a stranger. I was the only one who wasn't rolling!

"I don't get it," I said, throwing my hands up in defeat. "This drug is one fickle diva."

Molly must've heard me talking shit about her, because at that moment everything started to feel like fireworks. My brain turned into an orange that was getting its pulp squeezed out, my skin glowed like an orb, and anything I touched felt like someone was fingering my prostate.

"False alarm, guys! I think Molly's here!"

"Yay!" Jenny giggled, sounding like an excited toddler. "Let's go mingle."

Jenny and I bounced around the bar like two pinballs, talking to everything and everyone. It was like Molly had pressed the fast-forward button in my brain and given me the attention span of a gnat. At first it felt spectacular, but then it got a little too cray cray. I was over the music creeping into my bones and banging pots and pans against my brain. I just wanted life to go back to the way it was before. Unfortunately, when you take Molly, it's about a six-hour trip back to normal. Putting that pill in your body means you've made a commitment to being fucked-up.

Frazzled and growing more anxious by the minute, I hopped into a cab without telling any of my friends and hightailed it back to my place. The drive back felt like I was on a magic carpet ride. The seats turned to mush, the radio tickled my ears, and the big New York City skyscrapers looked like dancing Legos. I had no sense of time or place. Before I could lick my lips and grind my jaw, I was already around the corner of my apartment.

"Okay, Ryan, you made it," I told myself in a soothing voice. It was Saturday night in the East Village, which meant that *Details* magazine subscribers and their bozo girlfriends were everywhere. I tried to escape them by going into the bodega to get a bottle of water, but walking was proving to be a difficult journey for me.

"Must. Get. Hydrated," I whispered, making it through the entryway of the bodega.

"Hey," the bodega guy, Tommy, grunted at me from behind the counter.

"Hi," I whispered, grabbing the nearest bottle of water and plopping it down at the checkout.

Tommy took one look at me and said something you never want to hear when you're on drugs. "Do you need to go to the hospital?"

Even though I was sweating off half my body weight and could barely walk, it never occurred to me that I might actually need medical assistance. But if someone wants to call you an ambulance, it seems unwise to argue.

Tommy came out from behind the counter and made me sit down on a milk crate while he called 911. I couldn't hear what he was saying to the dispatcher, but I did catch the words, "I don't know. He just looks really bad."

Freaking out on Molly is confusing because part of you is going nuts with worry and the other part is just really high and happy and wants to suck on a lollipop. Your thought process is, "OMG, I think I'm dying. This totally sucks. Wait—who does this song? I want to dance!" As I waited for the ambulance to come, random drunk people stumbled into the bodega and saw me bopping my head and smacking my lips on a milk crate and burst out laughing. You know shit's bad when people who are barely conscious look at you and say, "Wow, that dude is fucked-up."

A few minutes had passed, and there was no sign of an

ambulance. Growing impatient, I asked Tommy what the holdup was.

"I don't know," Tommy shrugged. "You try calling them."

I found the concept of having to call my own ambulance deeply offensive. "No, Tommy," I scoffed. "You do it. It was your idea!"

Tommy sighed and called 911 again. This time I was able to catch the entire conversation. "Yeah, hi. I just called for an ambulance fifteen minutes ago to come to East Seventh and First Avenue. Where is it? It'll be here soon? Uh, okay." Tommy hung up the phone and told me to hang tight.

I was horrified. I had ordered pizzas that came quicker than this ambulance. Luckily, my phone rang and jolted me out of my half-rage, half-Ecstasy spiral. It was my friend Carey. I answered as a wave of love and appreciation crashed onto my brain.

"Hey, Carey, I'm so happy you're calling me right now! How are you?"

"Hey, Ry, I'm around the corner from your apartment. What are you doing?"

"I'm sitting on a milk crate in my bodega rolling on Ecstasy."

"WHAT?"

"The bodega guy thought I needed an ambulance, so he called me one. It should be here soon."

"An ambulance? But you sound fine!"

Carey was right. I did sound relatively fine. Sitting on the milk crate for fifteen minutes had chilled me out, and now I was actually feeling pretty good again.

"I know, but it's already been called. I can't just leave."

"Yes, you can. Ryan, ambulance rides cost, like, $4,000. Just leave now and I'll meet you at your place in two minutes."

Seemingly on cue, I started to hear sirens. This was it. I could stay and spend the night in a hospital or I could go home and watch Carey give me a DIY light show in my living room. I stood up from the milk crate.

"Hey!" Tommy shouted at me. "Don't go anywhere. Your ambulance is almost here!"

"Ryan, don't listen to him!" Carey yelled into the phone. "Go!"

I took a deep breath, mouthed an apology to Tommy, and sped out of the bodega. As I exited, I exchanged a knowing glance with an EMT who was coming out of the ambulance that was meant for me, and then I ran like hell toward my apartment.

"I'm running from the ambulance!" I screamed into my phone. "I did it!"

When I got home, Carey came over and gave me back massages and showed me fun visuals on YouTube. I went to bed as the sun was coming up and woke up later feeling like Molly had taken a giant shit on my brain and body. Trying to shake off the weirdness, I met up with some friends and tried to turn my terrifying experience into amusing brunch fodder. I was good at this: processing something humiliating and painful and then turning it into everyone else's pleasure. My friends laughed uproariously at my story, especially when I told them the part about running away from the ambulance, but I couldn't laugh with them and mean it. This fuckup had left a mark. When I made mistakes in college, they didn't hit me very hard, because everybody else was falling down with me. Things were different now, though. It had been a while since I peed my pants laughing as I watched a friend fall down drunk in the street or partied with a friend who made every amazing thing seem possible. Now it seemed like I was just trying to destroy my life. I didn't understand that if you keep daring your life to implode, it eventually will. I would, though. There comes a time when it no longer makes sense to do things for the story. All of the instances in which I tested my life by literally running into oncoming traffic, drinking excessively, and experimenting with drugs were going to reveal their consequences to me, and it was going to make everything leading up to it look like a piece of insignificant cake.

The Rx Generation

ONE OF THE HALLMARKS of being young is feeling like you're invincible. A twenty-three-year-old does an eight ball of coke in one night and chases it with a tab of acid because he can't conceive of a bad outcome. A young gay man has unprotected sex because he's convinced an STD will elude him. This, of course, isn't a sustainable attitude. Eventually you see the negative effects of your actions, and once that happens, you're officially on the last legs of your youth. It dawns on everyone—that moment where your life becomes something real rather than something for you to ash your cigarette on.

My breakthrough/breakdown came in the winter of 2012 after I had spent the last nine months stabbing myself with the hot poker known as "life experiences." If you stalked my Twitter or Facebook profile during that time, you'd probably think everything was going great. "Whoa," you'd say to yourself. "Look at this mature, accomplished guy who's going places! Will you please excuse me while I drown my sorrows in some peanut butter and jealousy sandwiches?" Although I'd celebrated my twenty-fourth birthday unemployed with no job prospects, so much had changed. I was now writing full-time for *Thought Catalog*, producing viral articles left and right and landing some cushy freelance gigs at places like the *New York Times*. Things were going swimmingly, or at least it looked that way. Like the rest of my peers, I was painting my existence very carefully, only posting pictures of me having fun at medium-fancy parties and sharing links to my articles. My life offline was becoming a very different story.

When I first moved to New York, I used drugs the same way everyone else did: to take the edge off a stressful week and escape into a carefree land of cotton candy and rainbows. There were times I overdid it, like the terrifying story I just told you about taking Molly, but the experimentation was largely harmless—that is, until I started palling around with prescription painkillers. Then things quickly went from chic to bleak.

I tried Vicodin for the first time when I was nineteen. A friend had some leftover from a wisdom teeth removal and gave them to me because they made her sick. At home I gobbled down four pills and thought to myself, "Oh. This is what drugs are supposed to feel like. I get it now. Coke, Ecstasy, weed: you guys can go home." It was love at first swallow, which is why I knew it'd be best for me to stay the hell away from them. Two years later, when I was hit by a car, I got put on a fabulous morphine drip for three weeks and was sent home from the hospital with a vat of painkillers. While it was tempting to say, "Fuck it. Life sucks so I'm going to spend the next year in a warm opiate cocoon of love," I demonstrated some willpower and only used my prescriptions to treat the physical pain.

Smash cut to a few years later: I'm holding down a full-time job and achieving some modicum of success. With every professional milestone I achieved, the urge to self-sabotage grew stronger and stronger, even though I knew this was not the time to fuck up. I could've done that in college when my only job was to find myself and hook up with boys named River from my Gender and Sexuality class. Now I needed to be smart and spend my free time doing yoga or whatever else healthy young professionals do. But I couldn't bring myself to make the smart decision. So I became a pillhead loser instead.

The first time I was introduced to my drug dealer it was in a social setting. In fact, I didn't even know she was a dealer, because she was young, pretty, and came from a well-to-do family. Her name was Olivia, and I met her through a few new friends of mine on a sweltering day in May 2011. The inconvenient thing about doing a lot of drugs is that you have to get a whole new social life. None of my real friends would ever be okay with joining me on a downward spiral. They had to meet someone for brunch or go on a date with their boyfriend or read their horoscope. Melting on the couch after taking three Percocet in some stranger's apartment at three o'clock in the afternoon didn't fit into their agenda.

Luckily for me, this was New York and I was in my

twenties. Finding kids who wanted to light the match and burn their lives to the ground was easy. I clapped my hands and there they were: my own posse of bad girls. Cassie, Maggie, Lily, and I had met in college. I'd watch them barrel through the quad wearing leopard-print pants and scuffed denim jackets, gossiping and chain-smoking cigarettes. *Who are these glamorous messes?* They were like modern-day Edie Sedgwicks, except they didn't carry themselves like little wounded birds. Their edges were sharp, and a single glance could draw blood. I had my first conversation with one of them in an elevator at the dorms. Cassie was wearing the same coat as me but in a different color, and she let out a half smile.

"Nice coat," she growled. Her voice sounded like it was permanently coated in whiskey and Marlboro Reds.

"Uh, thanks," I squeaked. "Got any plans tonight?"

She rolled her eyes. "There's this thing at Beatrice, but I don't really want to go. It's a snooze on Thursday."

Beatrice Inn was New York's modern answer to Studio 54. It was a small nightclub flooded with celebrities and various It Girls that came as quickly as it went. I'd been twice, but only because I was with pretty girls and arrived early.

"Yeah, I know what you mean," I chuckled. "It can be really dead."

The elevator dinged open and Cassie said good-bye before disappearing like a vulture into the night. "Wow," I sighed to myself. "She is, like, so awesome."

There had been brief run-ins after that, but our friendship didn't begin until I started to become undone. After graduation, Cassie and Maggie started a punk band that was attracting some attention. In a half attempt to be their friend, I interviewed them for *Thought Catalog*. I arrived at their filthy loft in Bushwick, and we took painkillers and talked about their music. I was elated. Even at twenty-four, I still wanted the unaffected cool girls to like me. After that night, we started hanging out on the regular, but it was always within the context of doing drugs. The day I crossed paths with Olivia, I had just bought Percocet from this freak on a leash named Magic Bobby and was meeting the girls at a park nearby. When I arrived, they were dancing on the grass and tripping on mushrooms.

"Oh my Goddddddd, so glad you madeeeee ittttt," said one of the girls, draping her wobbly limbs all over me. "Let's go get some alcohol and take it back to Lily's."

I said hello to Olivia, who was not only tripping on mushrooms but also limping. Whenever I hung out with these girls, something would always be askew, but no one ever cared enough to acknowledge it. You could walk into their apartment with a black eye and a broken arm and they'd just be like, "Cute sling! Do you have any Adderall?"

We went to Lily's apartment, which looked like a crack house that had a baby with a *Nylon* magazine subscription. I wondered what would happen if these girls ever took home a guy who wasn't a derelict drug addict. Like, what if Lily brought a stockbroker named Chad back to her apartment? He'd see her room covered in tin foil, coke straws, and glass pipes and run screaming. Druggies can't interact with the Chads of this world. They speak a sad language only a few people understand.

The second the girls sat down on Lily's dilapidated couch,

they started huffing whipped cream bottles. After those were drained, they all guzzled down beer, smoked some weed, took a few pills, and ordered coke from their dealer. I sat there stoned on Percocet, unable to process these tiny little blobs of white flesh in front of me. I popped another pill to help me not care to understand.

"Hey!" Olivia swatted me on the arm. "Where'd you get that?"

"Magic Bobby."

All the girls started laughing maniacally. "No shit; you go to Bobby? He's the worst."

Bobby *was* the worst. I had gotten his number from a friend of mine a few weeks earlier and was astounded by how bad he was at dealing drugs. He'd text you each day with what was on the menu: "Hello my little pockets of sunshine! I have my girls Mary Jane, Roxy, and Molly with me. Let me know if you want to link up!" I'd immediately text him back with, "Yes! Where are you?" but then I wouldn't hear back for two days. Or I would but it'd involve an all-day wild-goose chase across Brooklyn and Manhattan. Eventually I'd find him on some street corner, and we'd do the exchange right there in broad daylight. Sometimes I would be so desperate I would go to one of his rap shows and wait until he was finished performing to be like, "Great job. You really have star quality. Can I have ten Percocet now?"

"You should get my info," Olivia said. "I've got Percs and all of that other shit. Plus, I'm not insane."

"Oh my God, that would be amazing," I squealed. "Thank you soooo much." After I exchanged numbers with Olivia, I headed home. As I walked to the train, I looked at the clouds, which looked like scoops of ice cream dripping on an endless expanse of blue, and felt the last gasps of the Percocet making its way into my brain. I was almost sober by the time I reached my apartment and plopped my jelly bones down on my bed. I couldn't stop thinking about what I had just experienced. Any rational person would've looked at these girls' lives and thought, "Um, it's been fun but I'm going back to the land of boring normal people now!" but not me. This was only the beginning.

At twenty-four I was always one bad decision, one chance meeting, one pill away from being the worst version of myself. The opportunity to push the button and blow everything up in my life was always taunting me. When I made the decision to start going to a drug dealer and hang out with addicts, I was aware of the risk involved. I just didn't care. I had spent the last few years dipping my toes in the self-destruction pool, and now I wanted to go all the way and drown in it.

A few weeks after ditching Magic Bobby for Olivia, who was a much more reliable dealer, I decided to cut costs and go to a doctor for drugs. With my medical history, I figured I'd go in and say, "Cerebral palsy. Compartment syndrome. Ow," and immediately be given a prescription for Vicodin or Percocet. A friend of mine had recommended a Dr. Feelgood in SoHo who specialized in handing out pills like they were multivitamins, so I made an appointment that day to see him.

When I walked into the doctor's office, I was expecting to see a waiting room full of twitching junkies, but instead I found myself surrounded by crabby white girls named Amy wearing Isabel Marant sneakers and Marc Jacobs Daisy perfume. These were the new faces of pillheads: wealthy, irritable PR divas who needed Adderall to function at their jobs and Ambien to go to sleep.

"Um, where's Dr. Kearns?" one Amy barked at the receptionist while I was filling out an intake form. "I'm going to Europe for two months and need my Vyvanse and Klonopin prescriptions!"

"He's running behind today," the exhausted receptionist explained.

"He's always running fucking behind," Amy hissed before huffing off to take a seat.

After waiting for an hour and a half, Dr. Kearns was finally ready to see me. I started sweating bullets. What if he saw right through my lies and called the police on me? Or worse—what if he was just like, "No"? My nervousness abated the second he entered the room. He appeared rushed and out of it, barely looking at me as he limply shook my hand. Something in my gut told me this man wasn't going to have an issue giving me drugs.

"Hi, hi, hi," Dr. Kearns said, sitting down and examining my chart. "What brings you here, uh, Ryan?"

"Well, I've been experiencing a lot of pain lately . . ."

"Right, right."

"Because I have cerebral palsy."

"Uh-huh."

"And compartment syndrome."

"Yep."

"So I'm in, like, a lot of pain."

"So you have night pains from your compartment syndrome," Dr. Kearns said, scribbling in my chart, "and constant pain from your cerebral palsy. Okay, great."

I had only met Dr. Kearns for two minutes before he prescribed me sixty Vicodin with a refill. I continued to see him every few months after that. Once I asked for Xanax, explaining that I needed it for flying, and he gave me ninety pills.

"No, no—that's too much!" I protested. "I really only need a little bit."

"It's not like you're going to sell it on the black market!" He laughed, showing a rare display of emotion. "Plus, you can't overdose on this stuff. If you drink or take other drugs with it, sure, but by itself it's fine."

Having a Dr. Feelgood isn't just for people with a "drug problem." It's for all types of Millennials. While my parents were raised on weed and psychedelics, I'm part of the Rx generation. Many of my peers grew up raiding their parents' medicine cabinets to get high and discovered that pills are the perfect drug. Instead of buying them on the street, you can sit in a cozy office for thirty minutes and pick your drugs up at a Walgreens. Tell people you just took a Xanax because you were having anxiety and you'll hear a symphony of "Good call. That reminds me: I need to get a refill!" No one judges you. In fact, our culture practically demands that we medicate ourselves. We're on constant information overload, and the pressure to be "on" and perform at superhuman levels at work has never been higher. Using drugs to expand your mind and lie in a meadow all day is no longer relevant. We now do them to keep our heads above water.

In lieu of calming down with a glass of wine after a long day at work, I'd pop a pill, crawl into bed, and watch Netflix until I passed out. When you take painkillers, you go into this dream state where it feels like you're going in and out of consciousness. Your sheets feel like arms that are reaching out to hug you. It's lovely. You don't even mind not sleeping, because when you're asleep, you can't feel high and when you can't feel high, there's no point in feeling anything.

That summer, I began taking pills every day and thrived at work. At night I would attend some New York media party before rushing over to Olivia's shitbox apartment on the Lower East Side to take pills and watch some girl who was doped up on heroin do her makeup for five hours. I can recall that summer with a clarity that still makes me nauseated with giddiness. I remember sticking my legs out the window of my apartment on East Seventh Street, letting the hot summer air bathe my feet as I sucked on tangerine popsicles and listened to Charlie Parker. I remember taking Percocet in Sheep Meadow in Central Park and lying in the sun before walking the sixty blocks back downtown to my apartment. I remember being stoned out of my mind and making out with a dumb boy named Jake whose lips felt like a giant down comforter for my mouth to rest on. Life seemed perfect. Everything I had been taught about drugs seemed to be vicious propaganda. They didn't ruin your life. They enhanced it.

This is what drugs want you to think. They blow into your life looking hot as fuck, and before you know it, the two of you are in batshit love. Everything is great until it's not, and then you start to see the glimmers of instability and coldness. You convince yourself that this is just a rough patch and things will go back to the way they were in the beginning, but they never do. Once you see the cracks, you never see anything else.

The cracks started appearing in my life in October, maybe

November. Lily, Cassie, and Maggie all moved to California, and we never really talked again. I heard that Maggie went to rehab and Cassie became a dog walker. I have no idea what happened to Lily. Olivia was the only one left in the city, so I spent more and more time with her. Her apartment was constantly filled with pillheads freebasing Roxicet, a painkiller that makes Vicodin look like baby aspirin. The smoke always smelled sweet, like cloves. Freebasing had ravaged Olivia's lungs, and she kept a mug next to her at all times so she could spit up phlegm. She was only twenty-one years old. If I'd been sober, I would've taken one look at the situation and been like "XOXO, gone girl," but since I was high, I just thought, "Oh, this is fun and glamorous. Whose cups of phlegm are these? They're precious! You could sell them on Etsy and make a killing!"

My other friends had no idea my drug use had escalated. They knew I loved painkillers and sometimes would even do them with me, but they hadn't a clue I was buying drugs under a freeway at 2:00 p.m. and hanging out with people who freebased. It was getting harder to shield them from reality, especially because my behavior was becoming erratic. I'd experience these euphoric highs and then throw a giant tantrum over something as small as a long line at the grocery store. I had no tolerance for the unexpected. Drugs were eating away at all my coping mechanisms and turning me into a moody preteen.

At one point, I became paranoid that Percocet was making my face look sickly, so I decided to invest in the best eye creams, face masks, and colognes. I even bought a perfume that smelled like "Rich Lady Who's Going to Die Soon" and spritzed myself with it every night before bed so I could feel extra glamorous. Unfortunately, none of the products I bought improved my appearance. Pills had made my face so fat and puffy that I looked like Flounder from *The Little Mermaid*. It probably didn't help that I was also stuffing my face with chocolate bars. Remember heroin chic? I was heroin *not* chic. Opiates made me crave sweets. After taking my pills, my nightly ritual was a visit to the corner store for one giant jug of water and an imported chocolate bar. Then I would go home, lie in bed, and eat the entire thing in seconds. My roommate knew something was going on when she found countless chocolate bar wrappers floating around the house and opened the fridge and only saw "Hi, I'm on painkillers!" food like rice pudding, ice cream, and strawberries, but she probably just assumed I was stress eating.

When I wasn't binging on chocolate or moisturizing excessively, I was starting to nod off in public. Nodding off isn't like falling asleep. It's when you are so stoned you can't even keep your eyes open. Once, while in the throes of my drug problem, my family came to visit me in New York. We were all riding in a cab on our way to a museum when I started to take an impromptu nap against the window.

"Ryan!" my sister whispered. "Why do you keep closing your eyes and falling asleep? Is everything okay?"

Startled, I muttered, "Oh, yeah. Sorry. I'm just super exhausted . . ."

My mom was sitting in the front seat of the cab and stayed silent even though she knew I was on drugs. A few nights earlier, we were going through my bag looking for something when she saw that I had a bottle of Vicodin hidden in a side pocket. I took a deep breath and prepared to make up some lie about how the pain from my compartment syndrome had come back, but luckily I didn't have to. Instead of confronting me, she just zipped up my bag and asked me where I'd like to go to dinner. My dad did the same thing. Whenever I visited him in California, I'd take entire bottles of painkillers from his medicine cabinet. When I'd be back in New York, he'd call me and I'd think, "This is it. This is when my dad realizes I've been taking all the pills and I have to come clean." But he never said a damn thing.

I don't blame my parents for looking the other way. I was an adult living a separate life from them in New York. My issue with drugs was my issue only, and nothing they did could've changed anything. It is fascinating, though, to witness the level of denial some parents can have about their children. They remember the trophies, the stellar report cards, the nice boyfriend you bring home for Christmas, but they choose to forget the churlish attitude and the long stretches of unemployment and the bill from the STD clinic that shows up on the shared health insurance plan. Whenever I went home for the holidays, I played a version of myself that I knew my parents would like. I gave them their special boy even when their special boy was taking all their drugs and acting like a demon. Being fucked-up is an inconvenient truth many people like to ignore. We live in a culture that's only interested in self-improvement. The girl who sleeps her way through her twenties and does all the drugs secretly wants to be the first person to settle down just so she can show the world how far she's come. The workaholic stress case reads *Keep Calm and Carry On*, tries yoga, and turns into a completely different person. Hooray! People are constantly trying to shake off any qualities that could be perceived as messy. We want to deny that there's any part of us that could take pleasure in the wrong things when the fact is that you can experience true comfort in destroying yourself.

On December 31, 2011, I reached a new low in my drug use when I decided to take a bunch of Percocet and almost slept through my New Year's Eve plans. Earlier in the day, I had gone out to eat with a friend and kept accidentally nodding off in the restaurant. I apologized for being "so sleepy" and went home with the intention of taking a nap before getting ready for the night's festivities, but the drugs had other plans. When I woke up from my nap, I looked at my phone and saw that it was 10:45 p.m. I was supposed to be at a house party an hour before. Panicked, I called up my friend.

"Hey. I'm sorry. I took a disco nap and I guess it accidentally bled into '90s grunge." *Please laugh. Please never figure out how much of a mess I've become.*

"How the hell did that happen, Ryan? It's New Year's Eve—the one night a year where being on time is kind of crucial."

"I know, I know, but I'm on my way." I threw on some clothes, ran the fifteen blocks to the party, and showed up right before the clock struck midnight. When I opened the door, I was unnerved by how joyous the mood was. People were dressed to the nines and bubbling with energy. They were acting like they were actually happy. To save face, I did my best impression of a person who was having fun, and everybody bought it. By now I was an expert at acting normal and hiding the fact that I felt deader than dead on the inside. As I walked home alone from the party at 2:00 a.m., I thought of a perfect New Year's resolution for 2012: try not to sleep through it, you fucking loser.

I attempted to quit painkillers many times, but it never worked. I'd go to Los Angeles for a few weeks to dry out, only to end up flying back to New York early so I could get high. Or I would flush the pills Dr. Kearns gave me down the toilet and delete Olivia's number from my phone, which would last a few days until I got a craving and I'd send Olivia a message on Facebook saying, "Hey, babe. Someone stole my phone and I lost all my numbers. Can you give me yours?" When I was really feeling hopeless, I would attend NA and A.A. meetings, but it was pointless because I didn't identify as an addict. My only hope at getting better was to wait until something happened that would make me come to my senses and quit doing drugs for good. For many people, this rock bottom comes in the form of a horrific accident or an overdose, but I got lucky. All I needed was a limp dick.

Somehow, in the midst of always being on drugs and writing a billion posts a day for *Thought Catalog*, I went on a college speaking tour. Even though I had experienced some success as a blogger, I felt like a hack telling someone four years younger than me how to land a writing job. If I were being honest, my number one tip would be to take a bunch of opiates and write some sappy blog post about love. That's what worked for me.

One of the colleges that asked me to give a talk was McGill, a university in Montreal. I had never been to Canada before and was excited to visit, but I worried that my growing dependency on painkillers would prevent me from stringing two coherent sentences together, let alone inspire a bunch of students. Since I never went to these schools stoned—even a druggie loser like me had a conscience—I would binge leading up to the trip and then start light withdrawals the day of my talk. It was an idiotic plan (why would you send your body into withdrawals right when you needed it the most?), but rational thoughts had peaced out of my brain a long time ago.

I flew to Montreal in the middle of January. The weather felt like knives on my skin, and I was starting to wilt. When I got to the event, I realized that this wasn't some casual intimate setting I could sleepwalk my way through. I was speaking to two hundred people in an auditorium. My legs started to shake. Visions of me passing out or—worse—puking *Exorcist*-style all over the podium began to haunt me. But then something truly spectacular happened. As I started to talk, a sense of calm washed over my brain and I realized I could do this. I don't know how the words and jokes came out of my mouth but they did, and everything was fine and people laughed and they clapped and they got the person they wanted me to be that night.

After the talk ended, I planned on going back to my hotel room alone and letting my body finish withdrawing, but my friend Laura, who lives in Montreal, persuaded me to go out to dinner with her and a few of her friends, one of whom was named Sam. Sam was a beautiful pale-skinned gay boy with wispy blond hair and crystal clear eyes. During dinner, I avoided him because I was feeling shy and unfuckable. When you do opiates, your sex drive goes AWOL. Since your brain is experiencing a thousand little orgasms a day, you completely forget about the existence of real-life ones. I still had occasional make-outs with guys, but when it came time to actually get down to work, I'd be like, "Hey, do you mind if we just cuddle for ten thousand hours while I play the same Washed Out song over and over?" Even if I weren't feeling asexual, I'd never pursue Sam, because he was way out of my league. On the spectrum of attractiveness, I fall in the depressing middle. People like me aren't ugly, but we never get laid because of our looks. We need to razzle dazzle them with our personalities and get them appropriately buzzed before they can be like, "Okay. Sure. I'm horny enough to do this." Sam, on the other hand, could have shit for brains and you'd still be like, "That's so interesting. Let me see your cock."

After dinner, we all went to a bar. I was getting drunk, which was helping to ease my withdrawal symptoms, and having an okay time. Every so often I would catch Sam looking at me and assume it was because my face was twitching from the absence of Percocet, but then Laura pulled me aside and told me, "Dude, wake up. Sam is into you."

"No, he's not."

"Yes, he is. He just told me."

Seriously? I'm twenty pounds overweight, I haven't taken a dump in five days, and my face is doing an involuntary rendition of the Macarena, and you're telling me this megababe is interested in doing sexual things to my body? I couldn't waste this blessed opportunity. When someone attractive decides they'd like to have sex with you, you have to say yes. It's the law. I sat down next to Sam on the couch and talked with him for a few minutes. We both knew this was heading into make-out territory, so every word out of our mouths sounded like a stall until we could come into *each other's* mouths. Impatient, I took the plunge and kissed him.

Within two tongue thrusts, we were making out in the club like a couple of horny monsters. I asked him to come back to my hotel so we could spare innocent bystanders the sight of me devouring someone's face. Once we got to my room, we rolled around on the bed and did that dance where you're not sure if you want to commit to a full-on hookup so you blue-ball each other until someone either falls asleep or takes it to the next level. Sam didn't want to go to bed. He wanted to fuck and/or possibly give and receive a spirited BJ. He took off his underwear and revealed a dick that was so rock hard and stunning it could've been on the cover of *Vogue*. I started to take off my underwear as well, but then I looked down and saw something so horrifying it caused me to gasp. My penis was flaccid. I began kissing Sam, hoping that it would jump-start something down below. I grabbed his ass and stroked his dick. I even tried the old, reliable dirty talk. Still nothing. I couldn't believe it. I never had trouble getting hard before and I had hooked up with some legitimate gargoyles. Now I was with Sam, one of the hottest guys my penis had ever had the pleasure of meeting, and it chose to ghost on me.

"I'm sorry, Sam," I said, my face flushed with embarrassment. "I think it's because I'm too drunk or something. This never happens."

"It's okay," Sam assured me in a way that sounded like he actually meant it. "I really don't care."

The next morning, Sam woke up and instead of running for the hills, he spent the next few hours in bed with me. The trauma from the night before seemed to be erased from his memory, and now all he wanted to do was spoon and make out underneath the covers. It felt great. Lying there in bed, legs intertwined with someone else's, I realized that I was, for the first time in almost a year, experiencing real intimacy with someone. It was something I had willed myself to forget. I forgot what it felt like to wake up next to someone and put your arms around each other. I forgot about the terrible dry mouth and the morning breath and the hot air that sometimes accidentally escapes from your lips and lands on the other person's cheeks. There are people in this world who experience this sort of closeness every day, and here I was, shocked to my core over an uncharacteristically tender one-night stand.

I started to realize what I'd actually sacrificed for drugs. Every night of fun I had with the Girls on Pills gang, every stoned morning I spent writing some blog post for my job had all added up to me sleeping alone with a limp dick, and I hadn't even noticed. Pills are smart. They put me to sleep and then slowly robbed me of things in the middle of the night—so slowly, in fact, that I hadn't even noticed that anything was missing. They took away my desire to love, to feel joy, or even to show up to my best friend's birthday party. They took it all bit by bit until one day I woke up and saw that my life had become nothing but static.

Being with Sam, I felt myself wake up. For the first time, I didn't want to grab my clothes and run to my comfortable cave of isolation and drugs and the Internet. I wanted to stay and bathe in his affection. I wanted him to hold me tighter and longer. I wanted him to tell me I could have something real like this and that it wasn't too late for things to change. Each second I spent with him, I was able to see more and more just how small my life had become. I'd been deluding myself into thinking that all my new friendships and happiness were based off something authentic when they were rooted in being high. Nothing had been real. When you take drugs, you don't want to see things for what they are, so you choose to look at illusions instead.

That morning I realized I had a decision to make. I could continue letting drugs dictate my life and ruin my body and isolate me from the people who mattered most. I could keep putting fancy lotions on my face to conceal my rotting corpse and go to parties where everyone but me looks alive, and I could spend more time with people who don't know anything about me except that my favorite kind of pill is a 10/325 Percocet. I could take my parents' drugs and force them even further into denial, I could spend all my settlement money on pills and quit my job and become a full-time drug addict whose life is fantastic until they're out of drugs, and then it's a flurry of text messages and a lot of panic and a lot of anger and a lot of your body shutting down until you can get your hands on the poison that it's been running on. Or I could stop taking pills and have a life that everybody is entitled to. A nice life. A good life. Maybe even a boring life.

When I returned to New York, I stopped going to dealers and my corrupt doctor and slowly started to put the pieces of my brain back together. Making the right choice had never felt so satisfying.

People who have never had a problem with drugs sometimes have a difficult time understanding the dark places it can take you. But everyone has experienced a period in their life when you do things that hurt you simply because you're not interested in feeling good. You think "good" is for old people who don't know how to have fun, and all you want to do is see how much hurt your heart can take before it gets damaged beyond repair. You want to do reckless things like go home with an asshole because you're convinced it will reveal some important truth about yourself, a truth that you need to know in order to keep going. But the only thing sleeping with assholes reveals about you is feelings of profound emptiness and occasionally herpes.

There are people who are moving forward in life, and there are those who are letting everything fall apart. When I was on drugs, I remember looking at people my age and being like, "How is their life so functional?" It felt like I was given tiny adulthood quizzes every day and failing miserably. Something just did not compute, and the more time passed the more I'd feel alienated. In my sad little brain, I thought, "You can have your lame relationship and good eating habits, but I have my awesome drugs, so who's the real loser now?"

A lot of people feel the same way I did (and sometimes still do), and they deal with it by retreating further and further into oblivion where nothing can hurt them. Some never get better, but I was fortunate to be scared straight. When I really focused in on my life and saw the mess I had created, I said to myself, "Bitch, you did not live in a body cast, roll around in a wheelchair, have leg braces, get hit by a car, and lose function in your left hand just so you could take four Percocet and rub $200 lotion around your eyes. GET YOUR SHIT TOGETHER." I think part of the reason I did let myself succumb to a pill problem was defiance. Growing up with cerebral palsy and getting in my accident had made me into a golden child by default. Everyone was in awe of how I turned out, which created some unexpected resentment. People were banking on me turning my bad deck of cards into gold. But what if I didn't want to be an inspirational story?

I have since given that angsty part of me an Ambien so it could go to sleep, but I will tell you nothing is cut and dry. I'm not perfect, and sometimes, in the middle of the night, I find myself cozying up to a messier version of myself. I never punish myself for regressing, because punishment and shame are what led me to being that person in the first place. Every destructive thing I've ever done to myself has come from not having self-love and not believing I deserve a happy, balanced life. And that doesn't stem from entitlement. On the contrary, it's about realizing you're like everybody else. You want a partner who understands you, a job where you feel valued, and friends who will actually hang out when you ask them to. Once you register how damn similar we all are and that you're not alone on Crazy Individual Island, you can stop going blind from only seeing yourself. It took me a long time to understand this, but the second I did I was finally able to lead a life that felt meaningful. Now I've become a person I never thought I would be. I work out six days a week, I try to eat right, and except for the occasional bedtime Xanax, I don't do drugs. Sometimes my newfound maturity makes me want to barf, but I wouldn't trade it for anything. My existence, while less exciting, doesn't resemble a flimsy piece of trash anymore. It feels like mine. I'd been renting my body for twentysomething years, unsure if I wanted to make the commitment to myself and buy. "I don't know," I'd think to myself. "It's kind of a dump. Am I really a wise investment?" The answer, of course, is always yes.

Epilogue

My twenties are almost over. If I squint hard enough, I can see thirty. It's drinking a martini and wearing boat shoes and cashing a nice check. It looks happy and, more important, not so different from where I am right now. Still, I'm excited to be older. I never thought I would be. For a long time I thought that youth was the most interesting thing about a person. I can't imagine that thought existing in my brain, but it did. It lived inside me, a different version of me but still the bones of the person I am today. I want to give that person a kiss and a slap.

A few months ago I was looking through old boxes of stuff at my parents' house and stumbled upon my father's old journals. The entries span throughout his twenties, and in them he talks a lot about being nervous asking out girls and whether he'll get into the graduate program at USC. In many ways, it read like an exact replica of the posts I'd been writing for *Thought Catalog*. You could've transcribed his journal entries, posted them online, and no one would've been like, "Um, what is this shit? It's not 1975 anymore, bro!" Looking at what my father had written, I realized a comforting truth: being a fuckup in your twenties is totally timeless! Most of our parents may have landed a job, gotten married, and had kids by the time they were thirty but that didn't mean they knew what the hell they were doing. They were forced into adulthood too soon, which is why when so many of them got divorced in their forties, they acted like selfish kids. People like to throw shade at Millennials and pretend we're the first people to ever feel lost in our twenties, but the thoughts that hang over a young person's head have always been there. The only difference is we have a WiFi connection that allows us to broadcast them. The people who criticize us have apparently forgotten that. They forgot what it feels like to be twenty-three and praying that one day you'll wake up and know how to love somebody and do a good job at work and maintain friendships and save money. They forgot that when you strip people to their core and see what they really want, it doesn't look so different across generations. We all have stories worth telling. We all feel the need to connect via our shared experiences. That's called being human, not a Millennial.

Communication is one difference about our generation that I will easily cop to. The many ways in which we're now able to "connect" with other people have actually made me desensitized. I've become numb to pretty faces. I've become numb to jokes, to hobbies and interests. Everybody looks the same in a thumbnail. Everybody's interchangeable on an "about me." I think of my parents meeting each other in their twenties and hanging on to each other's every word because their world was too small not to. You didn't have the luxury of looking up someone on Facebook afterward and seeing who your mutual friends were. You needed to be present. This could be your one chance to be with someone you really click with. Chase after them. Get their phone number. Don't flake on the first date. Tell her that you love her. It isn't crazy. Love isn't crazy. You can't afford to not be brave.

When I think of how we socialize now, I get sick wondering how many great people I've missed out on knowing because I only gave them three seconds to prove themselves. Instead, I went back to me, always me, and relied on my narcissism to keep me warm at night. I hugged my bent arms and massaged my tense legs. This felt familiar. This felt like something that couldn't disappoint me. But all of this living gets hard to do when it's just for yourself. I'm learning more and more that this world was not meant to be experienced alone. Whether you spend it with friends or lovers, you must have someone there to inspire you to be better and force you to be accountable for your actions and to pour your love into. You can find that person! You can do whatever you want. I've spent so much of the last decade feeling like I was somewhere I didn't want to be and wondering how I could get to the place that would make everything better. There was impatience, a need for instant gratification that my parents and the Internet had engrained in me, but now I'm not so worried about what's over there because I'm content with where I am. Here feels good. I like here. Here likes me. I'm not fighting it. I know I will eventually find a lover and embark on my greatest project to date, which is a long-term monogamous relationship, but until that happens, I'll be okay.

I don't regret anything. And neither should you. You should remember all of it. You should remember all the time you wasted in your bed or in someone else's bed or at some bar where you overheard the same drippy conversations. You should remember how thin you once were despite subsisting on beer and pizza. You should remember all the people you tried to love and all the people who tried to love you. All the awful overpriced apartments, all the toxic friendships, and all the money you spent on things you can no longer recall. Then I want you to remember the moment you developed a keen understanding of what works for you and what doesn't. I want you to remember being comfortable in your own skin and not feeling like you have to apologize for every little thing. I want you to remember the first time you decided not to put the entirety of your self-worth in someone's careless hands. Because moments like those are the most valuable—instances in which you felt yourself no longer becoming the person you want but already being it. That's pretty fucking special.

Acknowledgments

First of all, this book would not be possible if it weren't for my lit agent, Lydia Willis. Her unwavering support, guidance, and endless rotation of chic Comme Des Garcon ensembles are what got this book finished. Also, thank you to Nora Spiegel for discovering my writing and telling Lydia, "Hey, we should meet with this dude!"

To my editor, Michael Szczerban, I still have no idea why you, a smart thoughtful straight man, decided to buy a book from a gay bimbo like me but I'm sure glad you did! Through editing this book, you taught me how to be a writer. Thank you.

Sydney Tanigawa and everyone else at S&S: Thank you for taking this insane (and delayed) book to the finish line and giving it a beautiful final shape.

To my wonderful agents at CAA, Chelsea Reed and Mackenzie Condon. You ladies are the best cheerleaders a wildly neurotic boy could ever ask for. Thanks for believing in my writing/ability to make you $$$!!!!

Chris Lavergne: You are my #1 freak on a leash. If you didn't give my feelings a home for so many years at *Thought Catalog*, I wouldn't be here writing this acknowledgment to you!

Stephanie Georgopulos and Brandon Gorrell: I love you guyzzz so much. We were like an insane throuple in New York. Also, Steph, babe? Thank you for reading all the terrible drafts of my book and giving me notes on how to make it less terrible.

Mike Chessler and Chris Alberghini: Thank you for plucking me from the blogging world and giving me my first job writing for television. You're a ray of beaming light in an otherwise DARK AS FUCK industry.

Mom and Dad: I love you two more than anyone else in the world. Mom, you are the best mom ever. You are so selfless and loving—a truly remarkable woman. Dad, you've informed so much of how I see the world. I AM OBSESSED WITH YOU.

Allison and Sean O'Connell: Thank you for being related to me and letting me talk about you in the book. (JK, you didn't have a choice in either!) But seriously, you two have been stellar siblings. Much love to ya.

My stepmom, Pamela Eells: You have been so gracious and kind and inspiring. Thanks for being one of my best friends and encouraging me in all aspects of my life.

Thank you to the following friends for influencing my life/work: Caitie Rolls (Ten years of friendship. You will always be the peanut butter to my jelly.), my #1 hon Lara Schoenhals, Clare Tivnan, Cailan Calandro, Molly McAleer, Bailey DeBruynkops, Braden Graeber, Renée Barton, Carey

Waggoner, Deanie Eichenstein, Kyle Buchanan, Tanner Cohen, Rachel Zeiger-Haag, Alta Finn, Audrey Adams, Alex Simone, Natalie Roy, Danna Friedberg, Caitlin Truman, Colette Kennedy, Beth Montana, Alex Sharry. My *Awkward* family: Jenna Lamia, Sarah Walker, Leila Cohan-Miccio, Allison Gibson Montgomery, and Anna Christopher. Kyle Buchanan, for making being gay less gay. Michelle Collins, Sam Lansky, Carey O'Donnell, Jeff Petriello, Adam Goldman, Danielle Reuther, my lil' brother Jason O'Connell, my grandma Darline Record, V Bar in the East Village, where most of this book was written, and also Alfred Coffee in Los Angeles. Special shout out to Easton Gym and Xanax for helping me maintain my sanity while writing this thing.

About the Author

Ryan has written for the *New York Times*, *Vice*, Medium, Thought Catalog, as well as MTV's *Awkward*. He currently lives in Los Angeles with his boyfriend, Simon, and their dog, Marty. (JK, Ryan doesn't have a boyfriend or a dog.) *I'm Special* is his first book.